AF394684

PATRICK HEIDE CONTEMPORARY ART

# **Hans Kotter** . *colour rush*

## **Artificial Light as Art**. Approaching the Works of Hans Kotter
### by Peter Lodermeyer

A hotel in Germany, not far from the River Rhine. I inquire at the desk if it might be possible to look at the work by Hans Kotter that I had read about being here. The receptionist, obviously clueless to what I am talking about, gives me vague directions to one of the upper floors. I go up and down the halls for a long time, searching to no avail, until I discover in a roomy niche three large, elegantly-proportioned objects on the wood-paneled wall. In the dim light I am unable to recognize much of what is on the front surfaces. I notice a light switch and turn it on, not suspecting it has anything to do with this object. There is a short flickering within the three upright rectangular boxes – and suddenly a veritable miracle of light takes place. Across nine square meters of surface a cascade of colour forms lights up in bright cobalt blue, yellow, and bottle green, undulating in slanted waves across one other. To the right the colour culminates in a magnificent cognac-coloured glow. The light-flooded forms remain inexplicable, like in an abstract painting, and at the same time oddly real, material, photographically precise. They seem organically animated – and yet their colours are so cool, their appearance so smooth, that they maintain an air of something confusingly foreign and inapproachable.

Confronted out of the blue with Hans Kotter's photographic works, oscillating between abstraction and materiality, naturalness and artificiality, technical perfection and painterly appearance, a person will inevitably question whether or not these are phenomena that have been digitally produced or altered. The truth of the matter is that the artist takes his camera, zooming in on drops of oil or glass prisms he has built himself in order to observe there the confusingly complicated play of the refraction, diffraction, and reflection of light. Through skillful lighting from various sources, forms of strange beauty and splendid colour quality emerge in the interior of these transparent media. During this process, transitions that are difficult to identify even though they result from light-flooded matter, colourful backgrounds and reflecting surfaces, create phenomena which evoke corporeal impressions, but do not materialize to any comprehensible shape. Thus, pseudo-organic formations come about that seem like paradox plants or landscapes made of fluids, and yet remain at the same time, immaterial, energetic, and indefinable in their innermost. These forms, which Kotter then exhibits as laser-chrome prints or slides in light boxes, are not subsequently altered digitally; on the contrary, they are presented in the way they revealed themselves to his camera.

Kotter's theme is light. His works always address light, tracing its most-unexpected effects. In doing so, the diversity of the light phenomena allows the artist to break fresh ground in finding highly varied possibilities of expression and ever-new techniques, materials, and manners of presentation, which extend beyond the customary boundaries of the genre. Hans Kotter not only constructs light boxes, he also builds objects, pours things he has found into transparent resins, marks entire rooms with paths of light made of luminescent foils, and, using his camera, approaches the most subtle phenomena of light. In conversation he refers to his photographic works as "painting with light", pointing out that he only discovered photography as an aid after much experimentation and mostly by chance. Kotter is not primarily a photographer, but an artist of light. As such, he is also necessarily an artist of space, since space reveals itself to us visually as a void that contains light. Not only his room installations, but also his light boxes lit with neon tubes reveal a presence that has a considerable effect on the room, and in fact, changes it. For this reason, it comes as no surprise that he repeatedly receives commissions for large-format installations in public spaces and office buildings.

It is highly interesting that a connection has been made between these light boxes and the windows of gothic cathedrals. What is diaphanous, i.e. the penetration of light through transparent matter, as well as the flooding of light into a room were often considered by art historians as an expression of the medieval metaphysics of light. The magic of the diaphanous certainly also occupies Hans Kotter in his photographic experiments, but it should not be overlooked that the artist is also aware of the fact that today our relationship to light is deeply profane. In his forays into the microcosm of optics he does not succumb to the abstract beauty of the light effects he has observed. He is too much the critical contemporary for this, acutely aware that the notions of light anchored in western thought as symbols of the divine, of truth and of reason have long since been subjected to a far-reaching secularization and finally, a drastic trivialization. One of the preconditions of the western metaphysics of light was no doubt, for the most part, the unavailability of the sun as it sought its natural course through the day and year. With electricity light became a constantly available, producible, and manageable quantity. For all of us artificial light has become a self-evident prerequisite of our modern everyday life. At night, thanks to the glow of neon advertisements, the headlights of cars, and streetlights, even the ugliest city can share in the profane magic of artificial light. At the latest with Dan Flavin's installations of fluorescent tubes in the 1960s, artificial lighting had become at once the theme and the "material" of a new artistic genre, the art of light.

In Kotter's installations and light boxes, the forms and mirror-smooth objects flooded with light always seem "sparkling clean and pure", as the self-ironic title of an exhibition of 1999 suggested. This motto that sounds like some kind of advertising can serve as a reminder that the western metaphysics of light has fallen today into the hands of product designers and advertising agents with their questionable promises of happiness. All of us are familiar with ads where the sun always shines and each tile, each chrome and paint surface gleams, where cavity-free teeth sparkle in their hygienically perfect condition, and metallically-painted limousines shoot across the pictures like beings from other spheres, silent and in utterly pure perfection. Hans Kotter's works consciously place themselves optically in seductive, almost flirtatious, proximity to the aesthetics of the consumer products that are perfect and sterile alike. Light boxes, the way Kotter uses them, are known to us outside the context of art, above all as an advertising means used in department stores and fashion boutiques. And in his installation "The very Best ..." he makes everyday objects from the sports world, a table-tennis table, and club trophies, gleam in a cold splendor that emphasizes the material. By exaggerating the sleek design, imbuing it with an alienating effect through his use of light, the objects are enhanced ironically, mutated to become "cool" signs of themselves with no utilitarian value. A turning of aesthetics into fetishes may be sensed in the table-tennis table, transparent and lit from below, but not usable for playing. Although its measurements correspond precisely to the measurements required in tournaments, the table-top contains a water-and-oil-mixture that would make a real table-tennis ball stick upon contact. Is uselessness a price one pays for beauty? In his works Kotter tests the borders of the narrow line between art and design, between beauty and functionality. Likewise, his light boxes, hung on or leaned against the wall, alternate between the status of minimalist sculpture and chic design object. But as soon as one activates their fluorescent tubes hidden in their interiors they become magic lanterns that reveal haunting pictures from the wonderland of light. Kotter's works are etudes of the inexhaustible fascination with light.

Translated by Elizabeth Volk

**Organic Colour** . 2007 . Stainless Steel Light Box . Laserchrome Slide on Plexiglass . 125 x 125 cm . Patrick Heide Contemporary Art . London

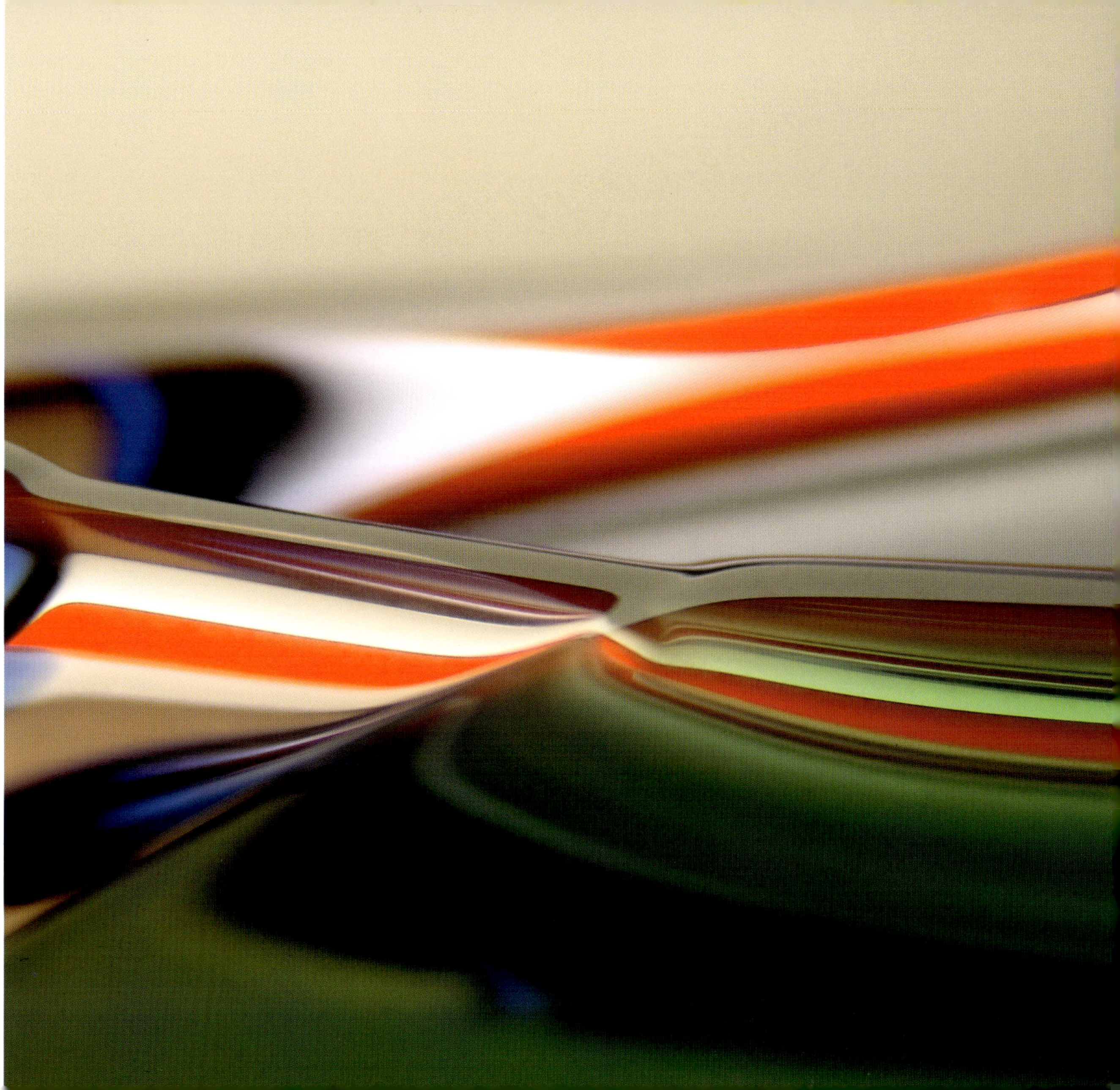

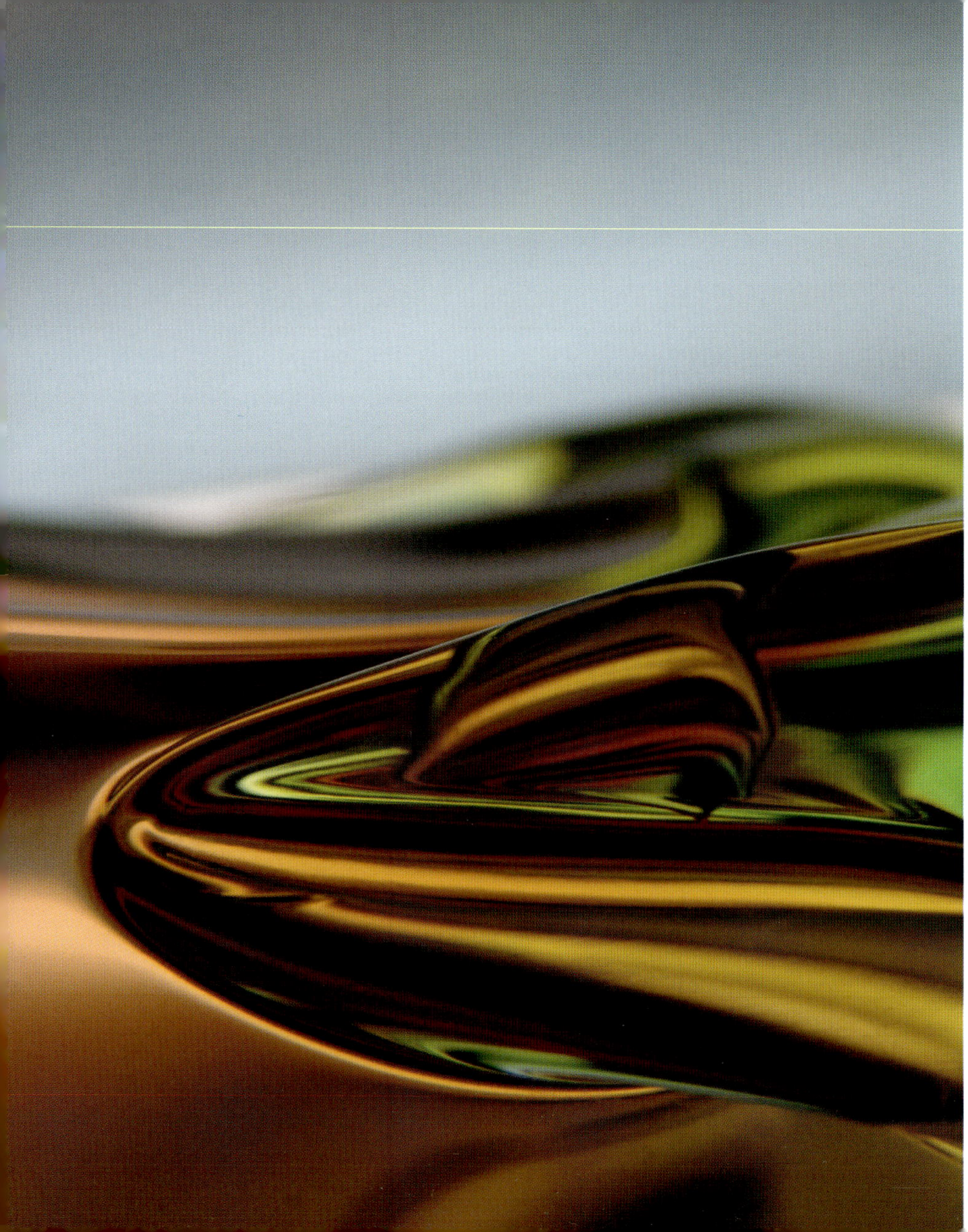



**Organic Colour** . 2007
C-Print on Dibond with Diasec Face
Patrick Heide Contemporary Art . London

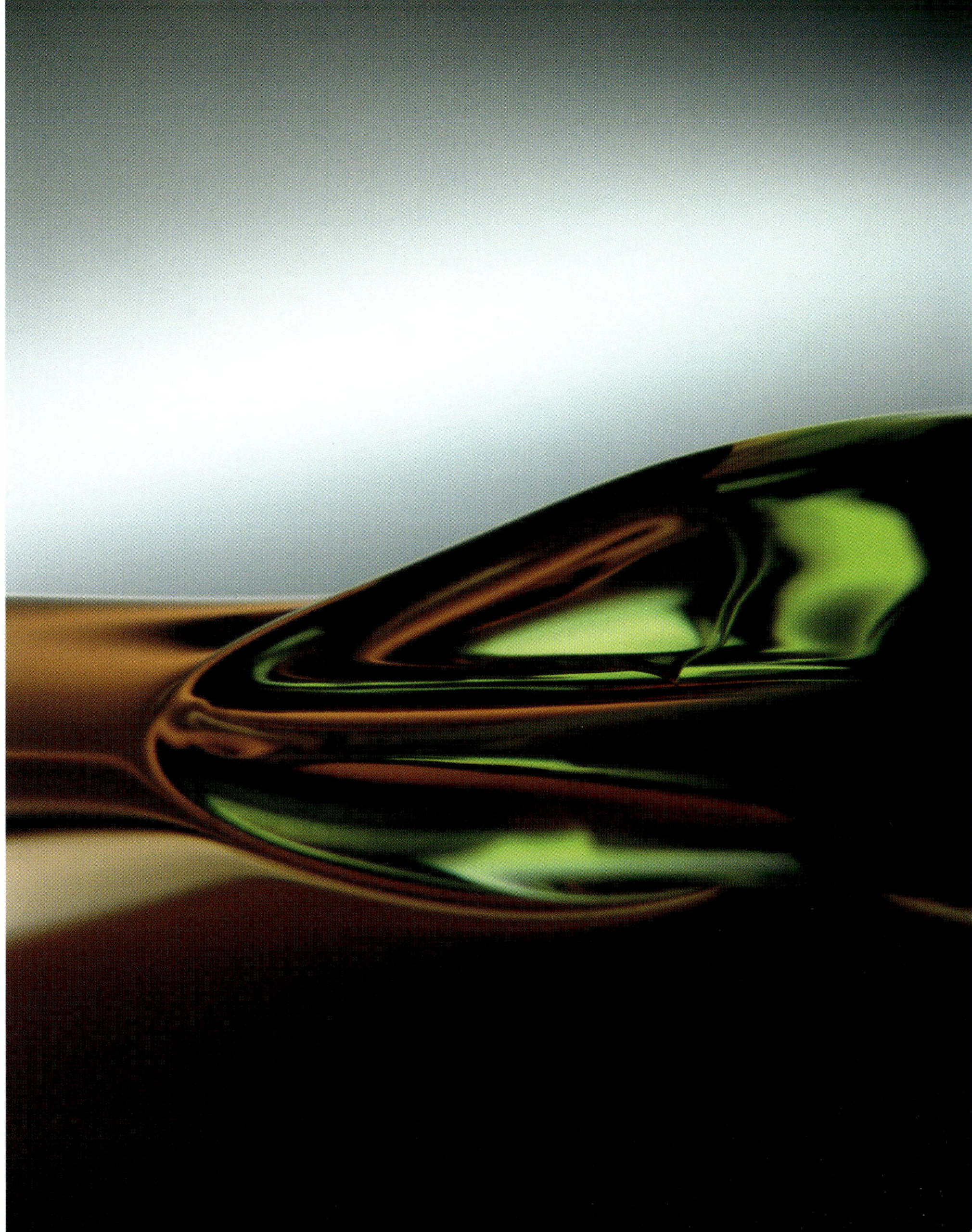

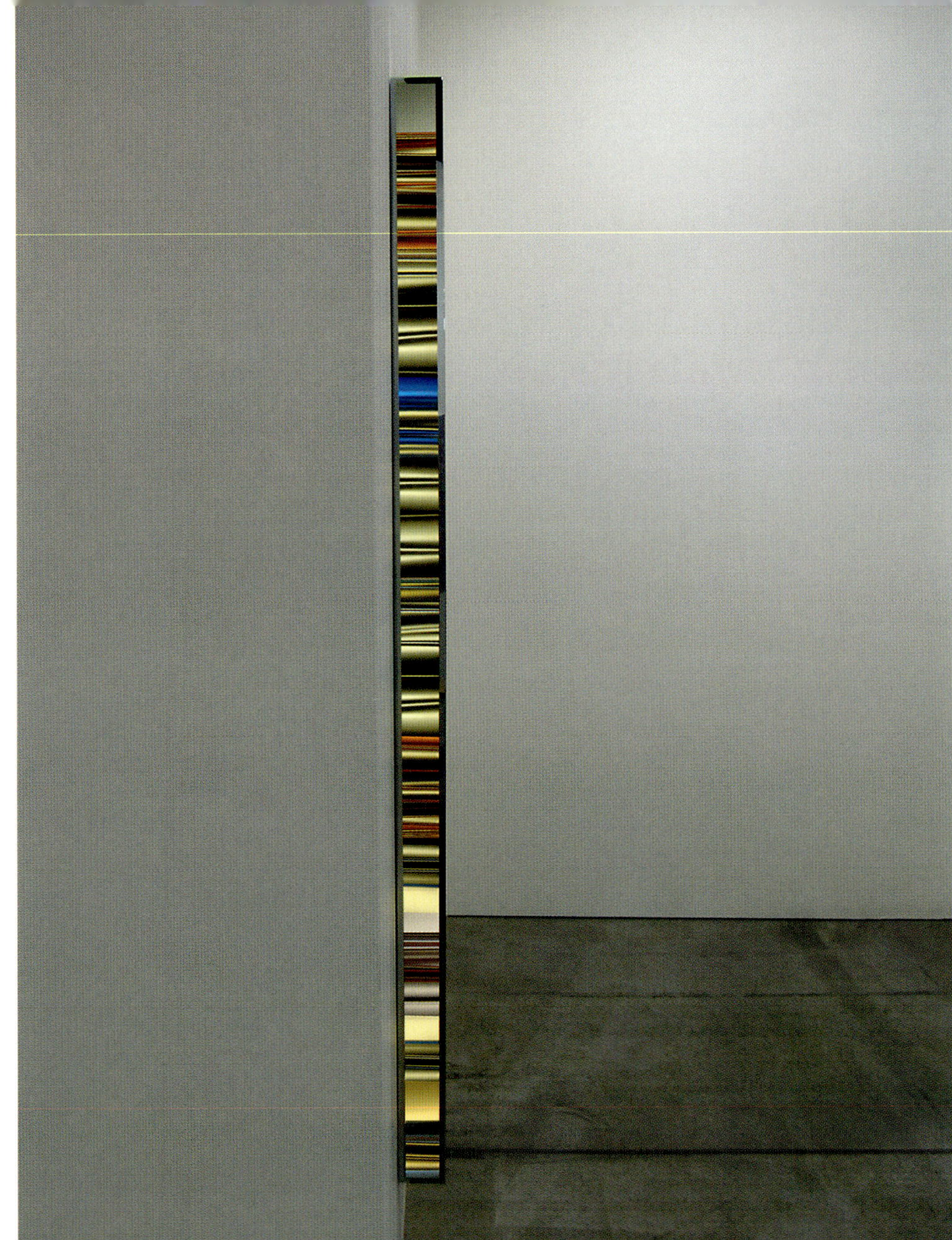

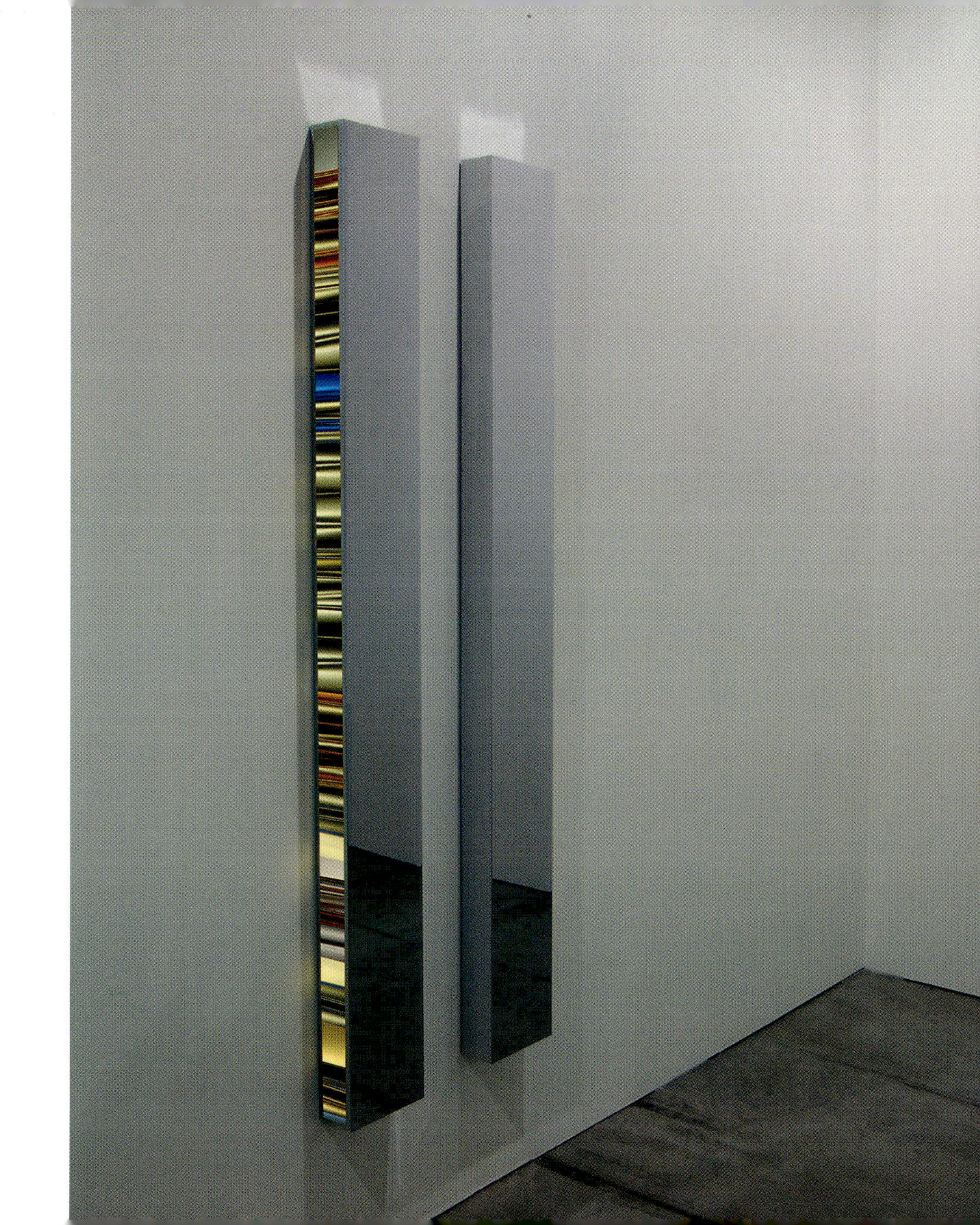



**Twin** . 2007
Chrome Light Boxes . Laserchrome Slide on Plexiglass
Each 190 x 20 x 8 cm
Patrick Heide Contemporary Art . London

**Sensitive Balance** . 2007 . Obsession through Technique . Plexiglass . Blue Silicon Oil . Water . Metal . Each 50 x 50 cm . ArtMbassy . Berlin

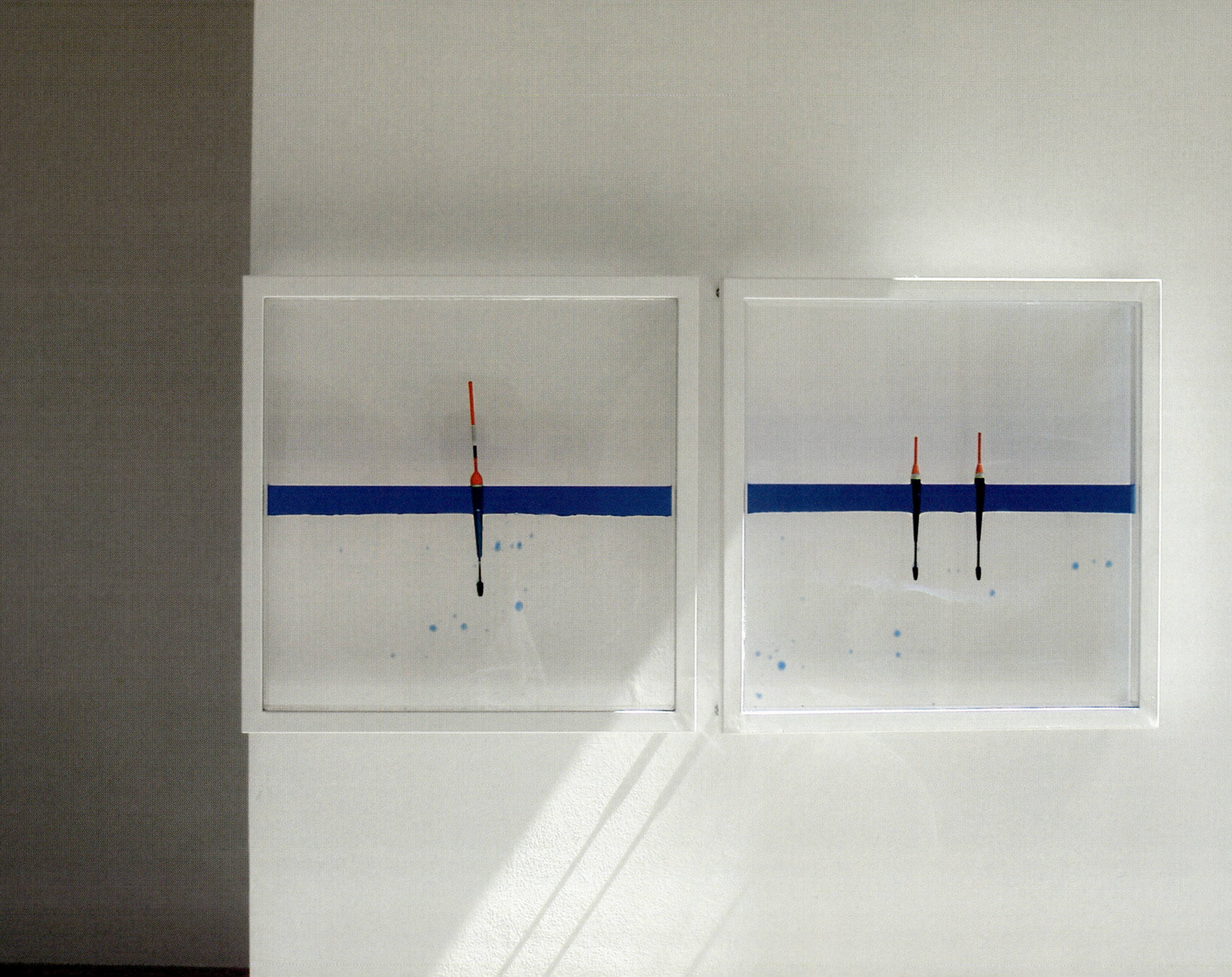

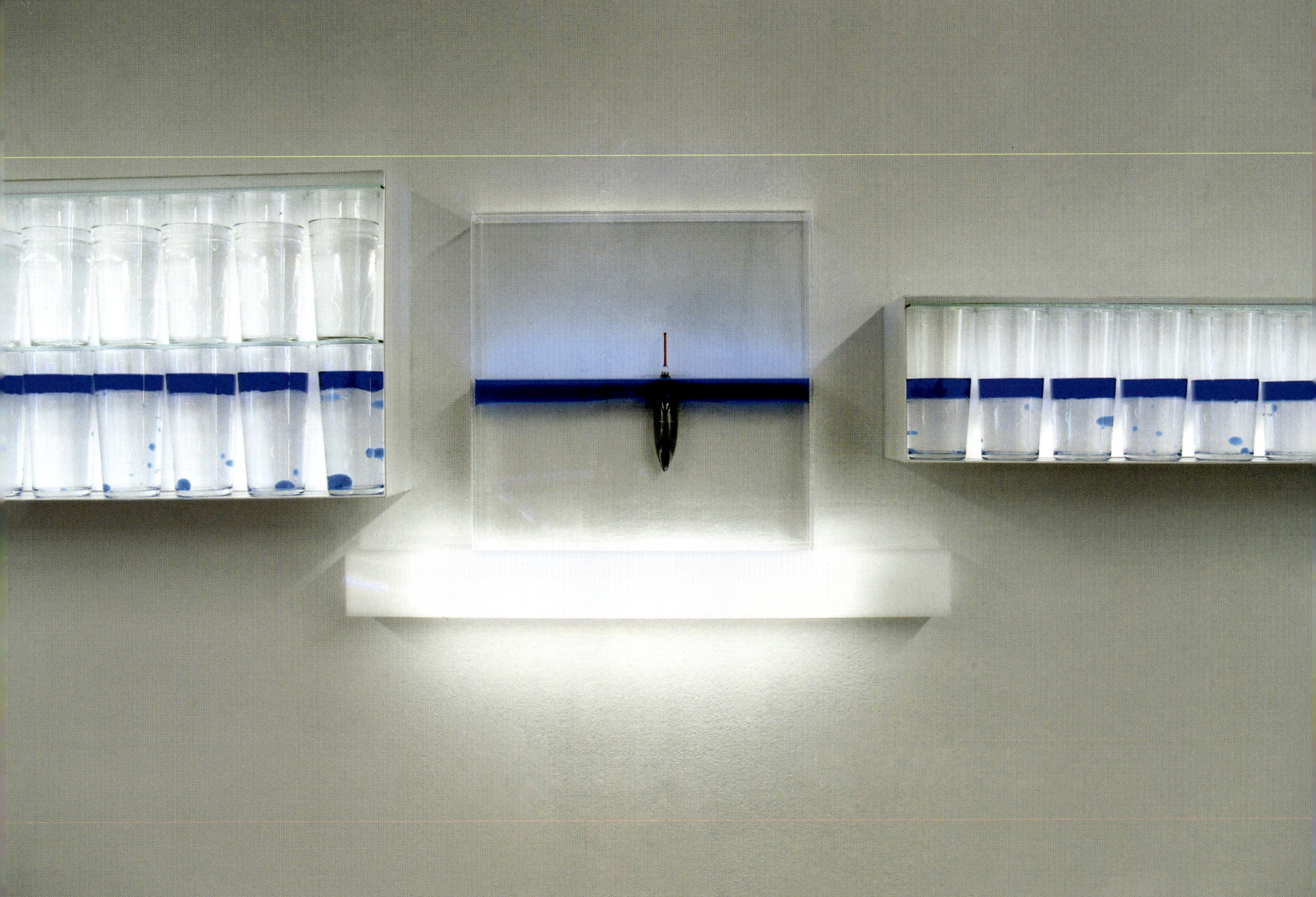

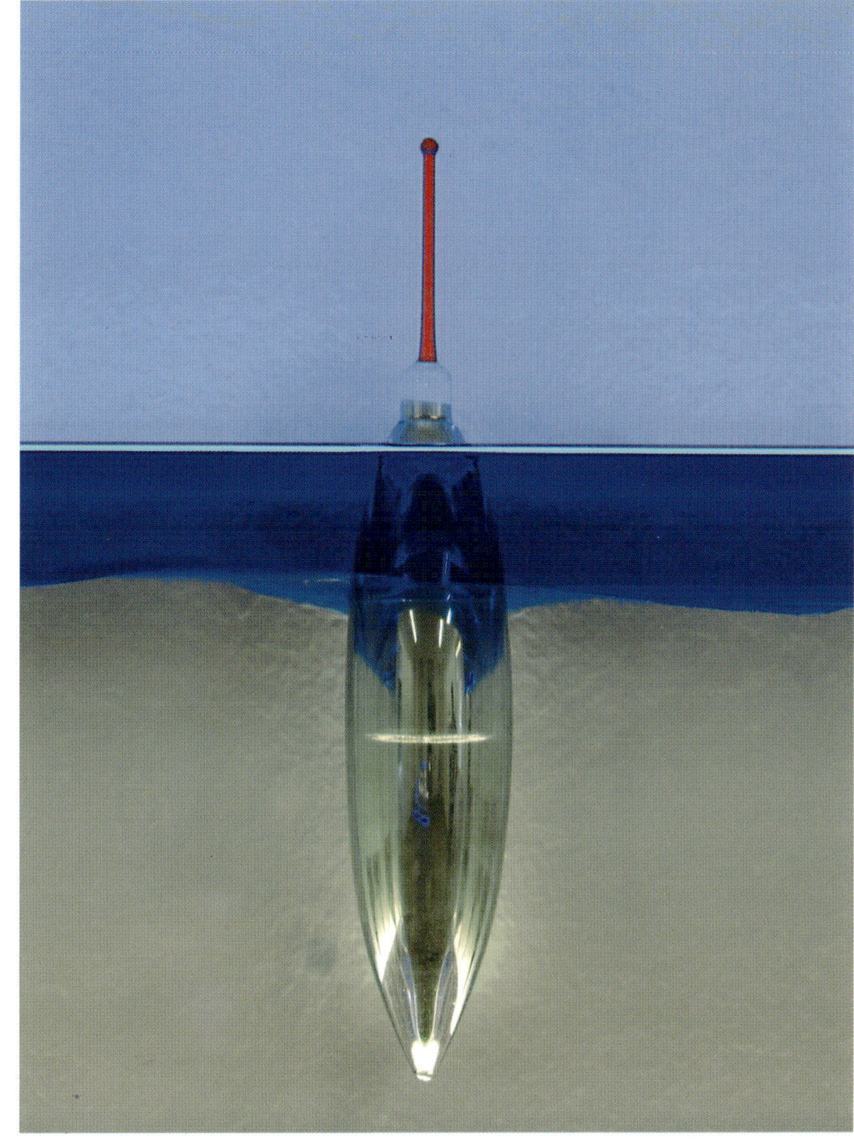

## 7

**The very Best** ...... . 2007
Plexiglass . Blue Silicon Oil . Water
High Gloss Polished Stainless Steel . Glasses . Cups
Best Before . Kunstverein Aschaffenburg

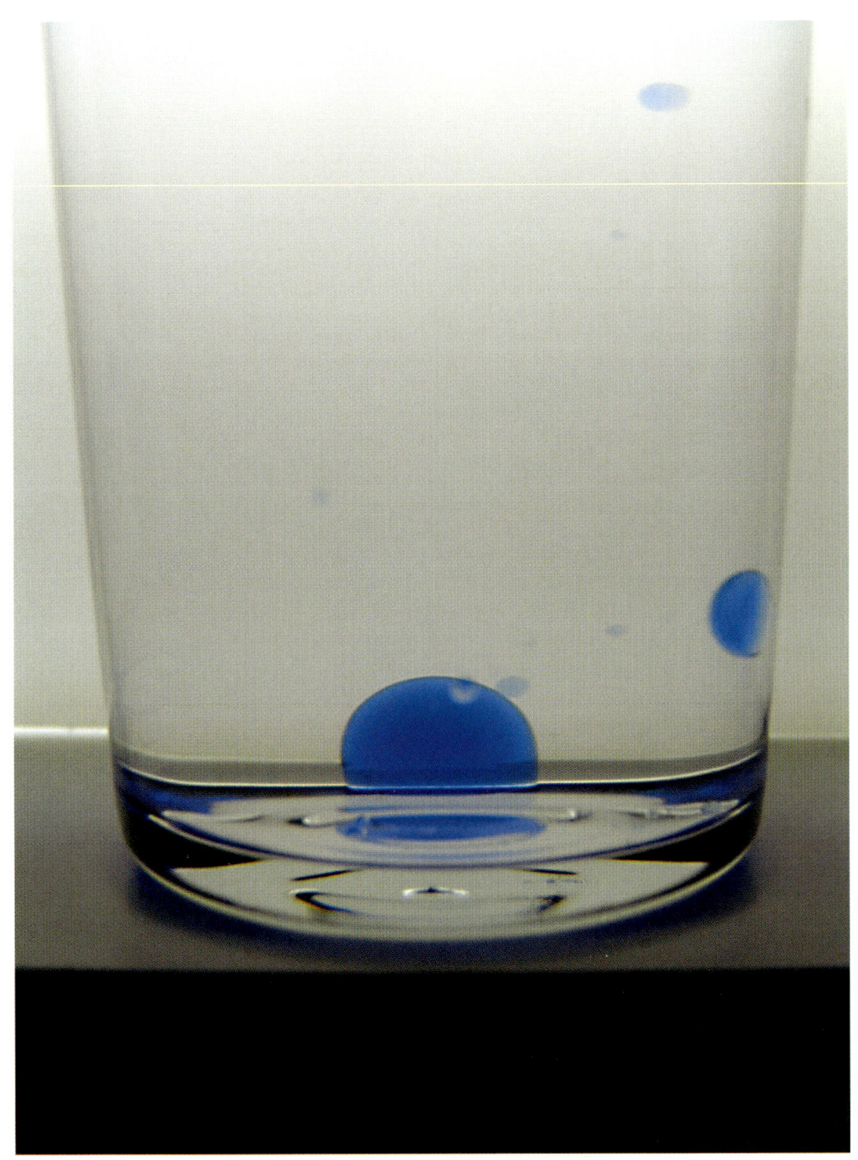

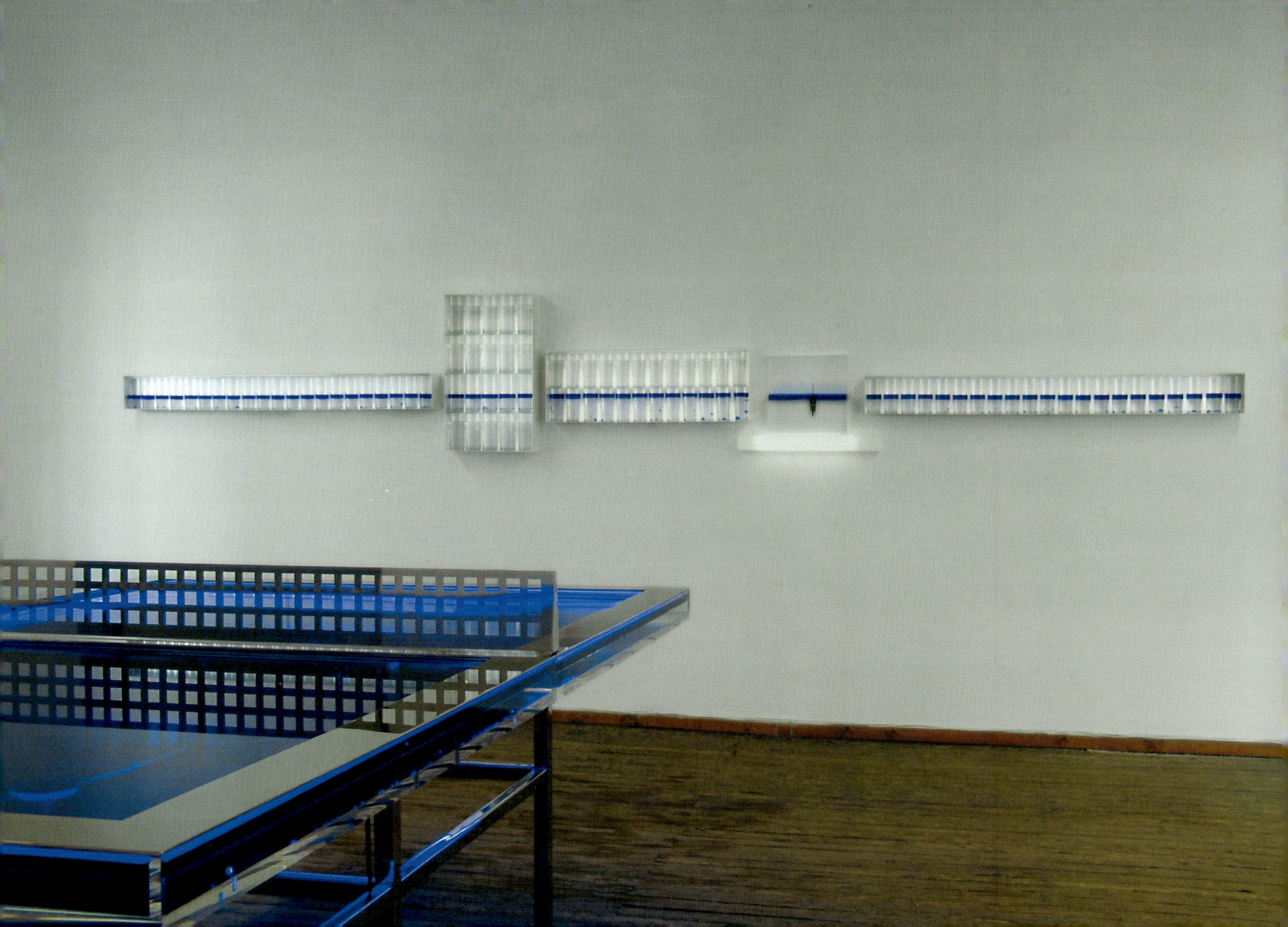

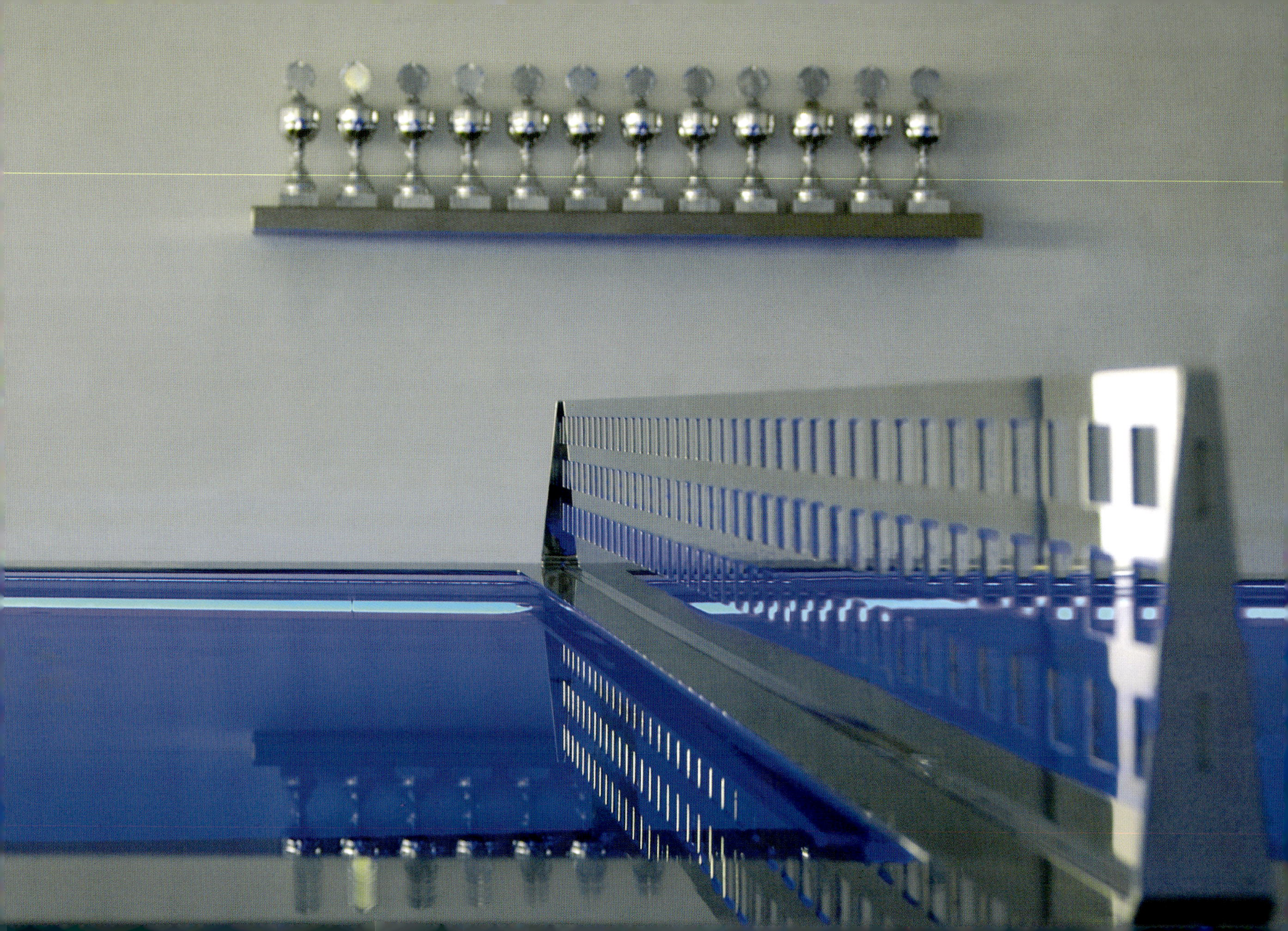

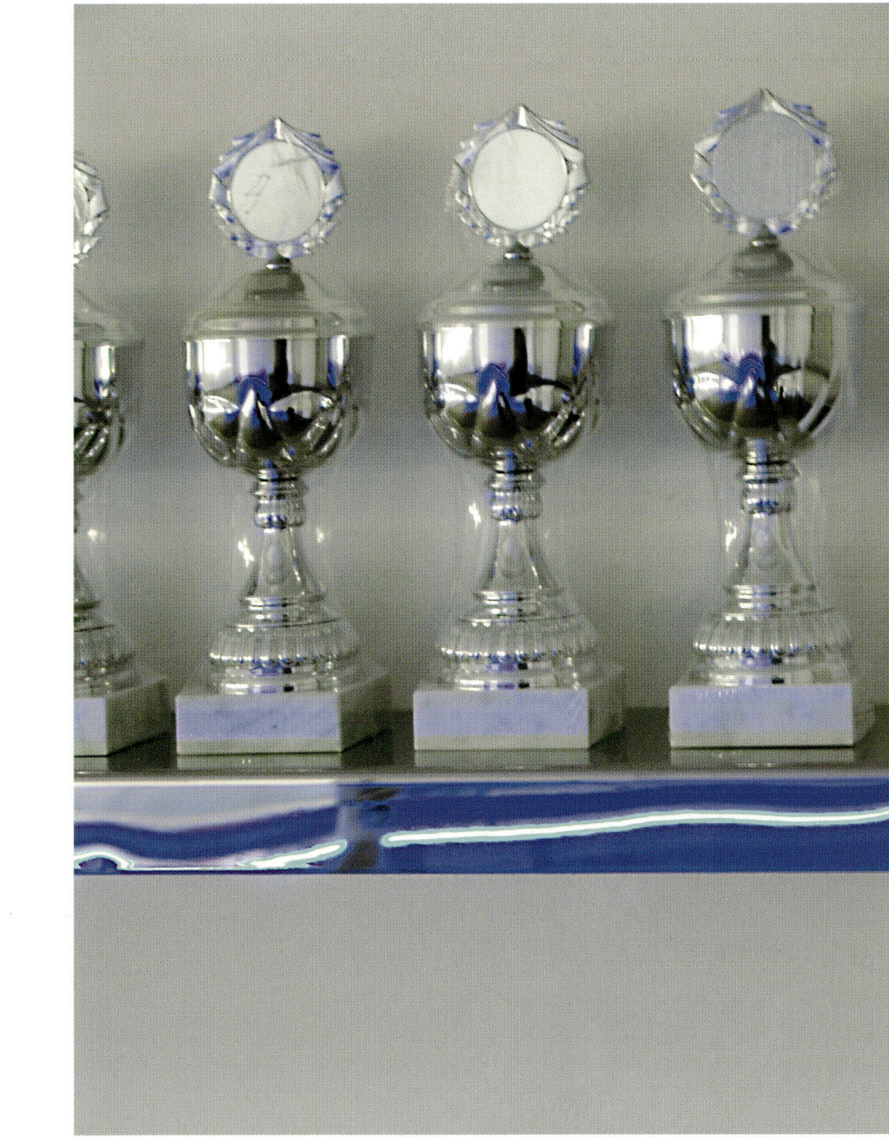

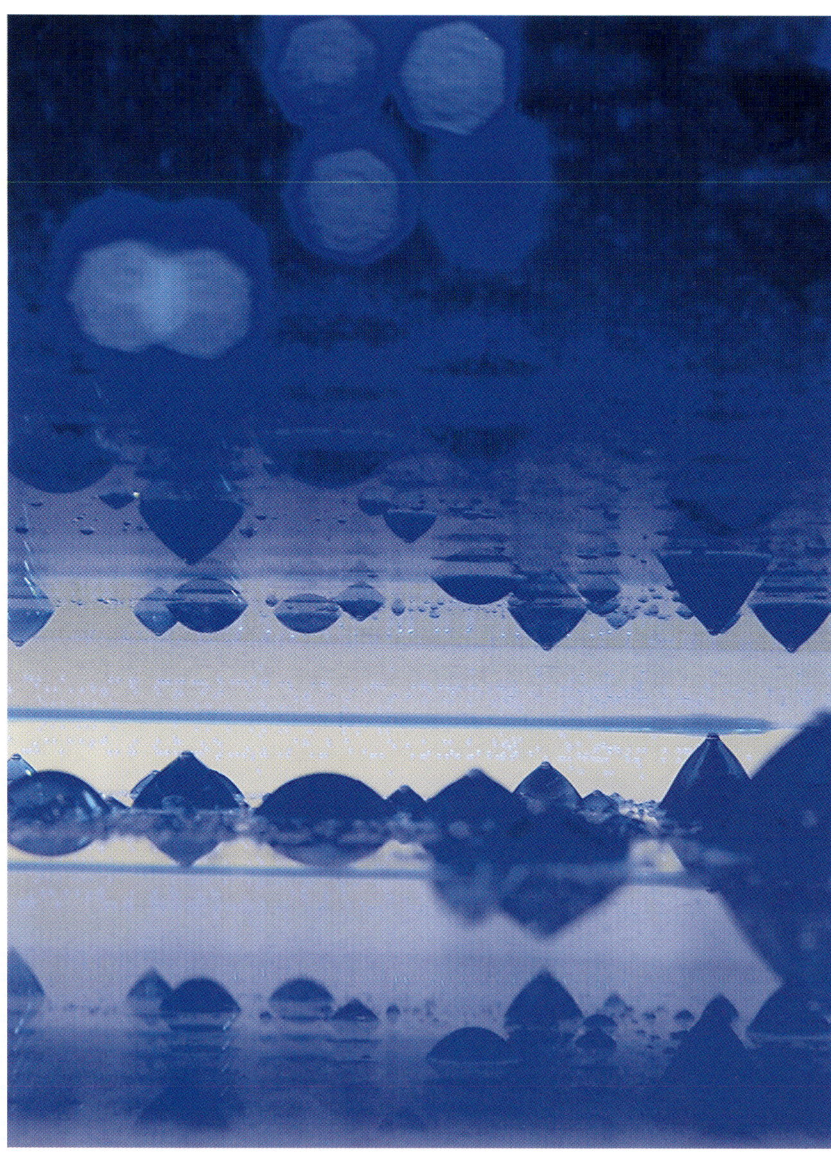

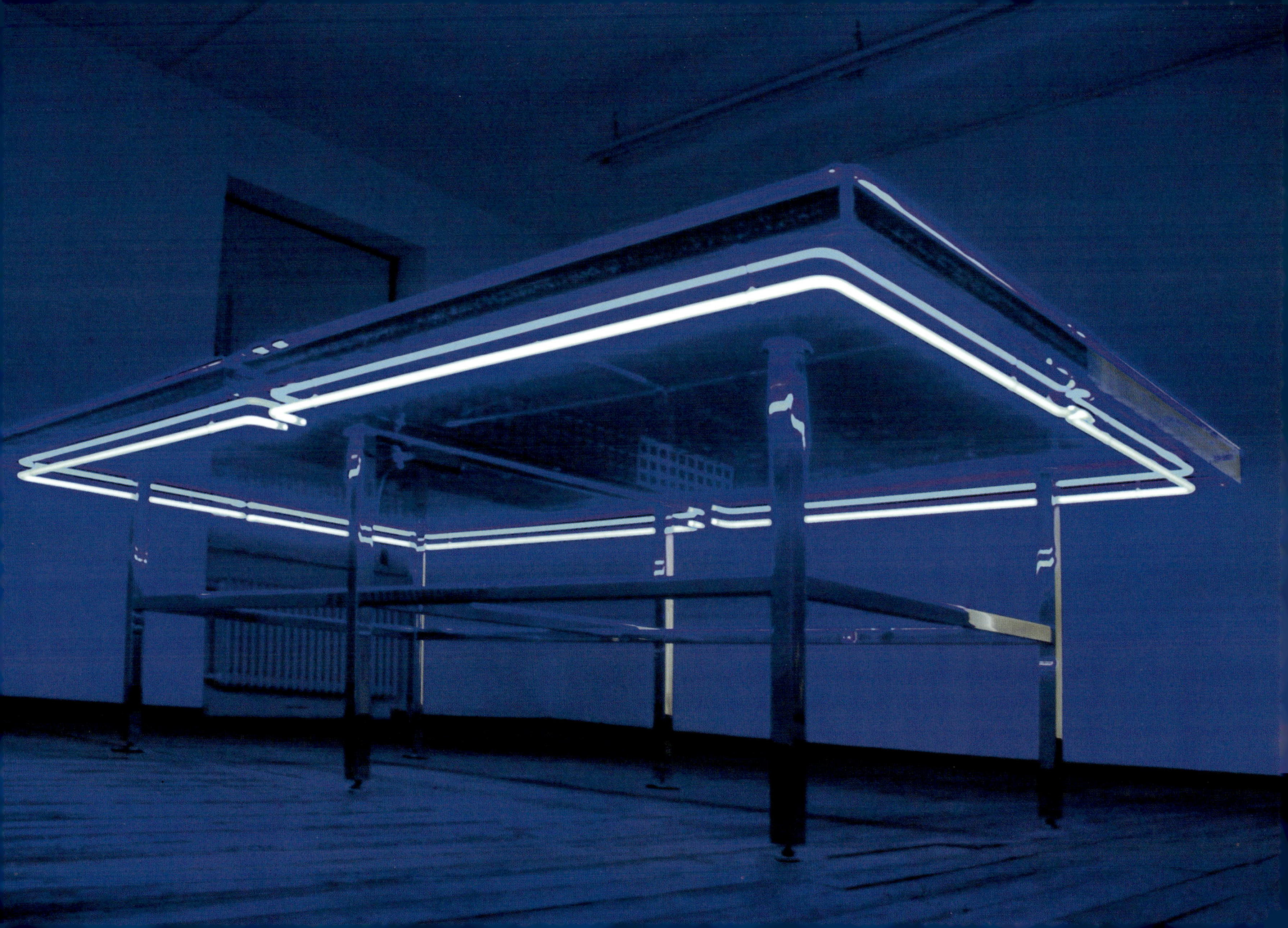

**Chromatic Plants** . 2006 . C-Print on Dibond with Diasec Face . Yellow / Green . Each 40 x 240 cm . Gallery Bernd A. Lausberg . Düsseldorf

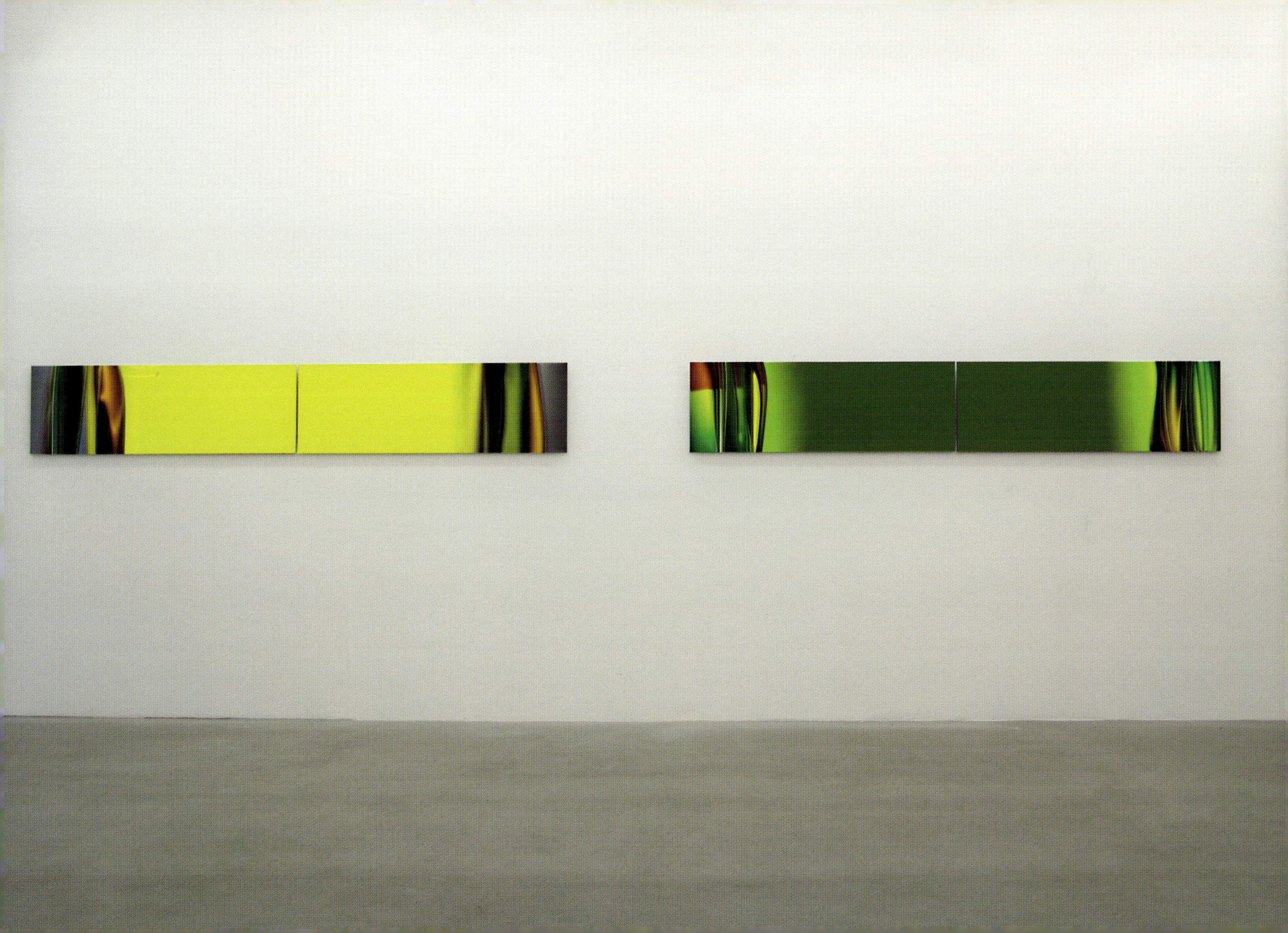

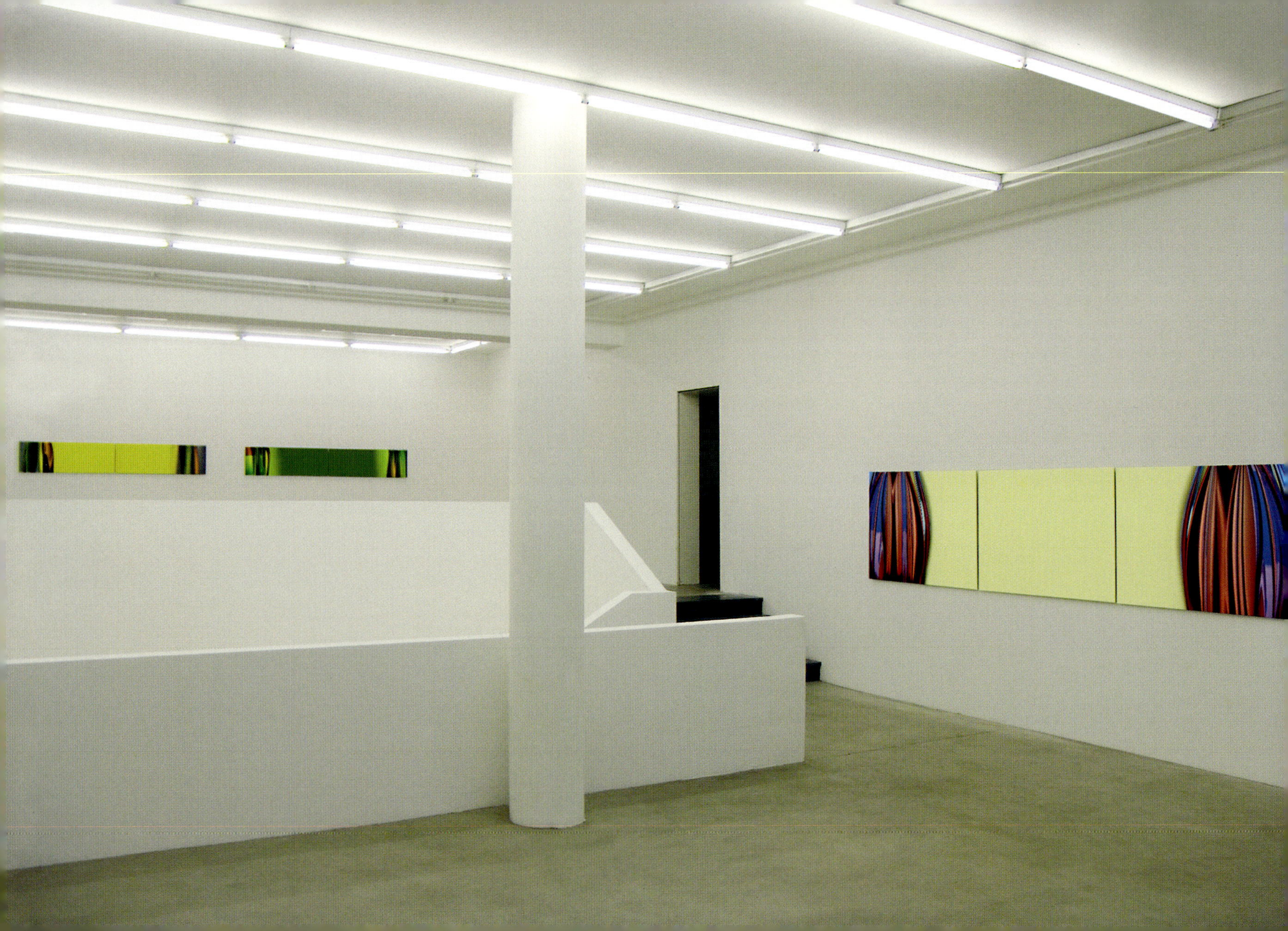

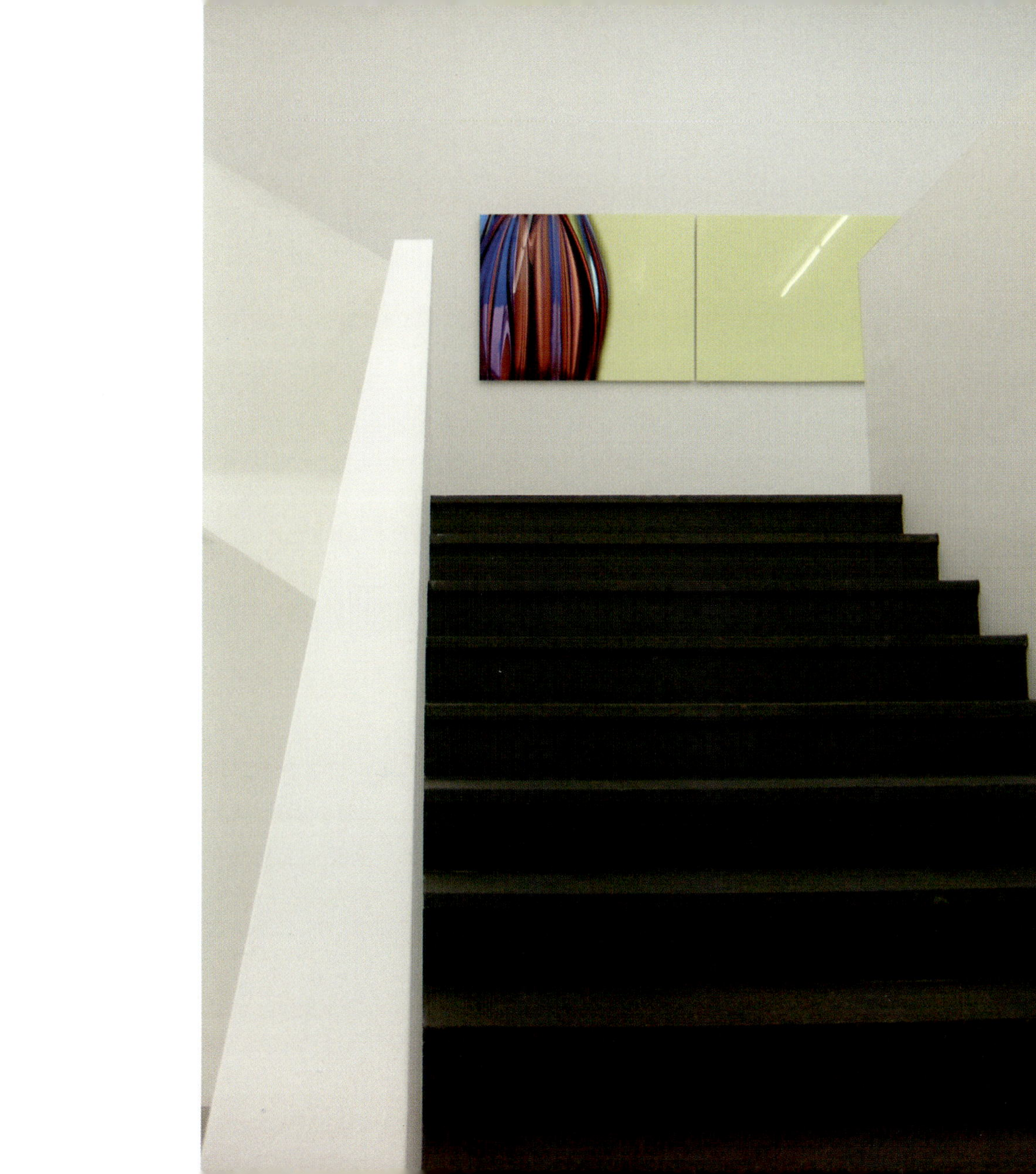

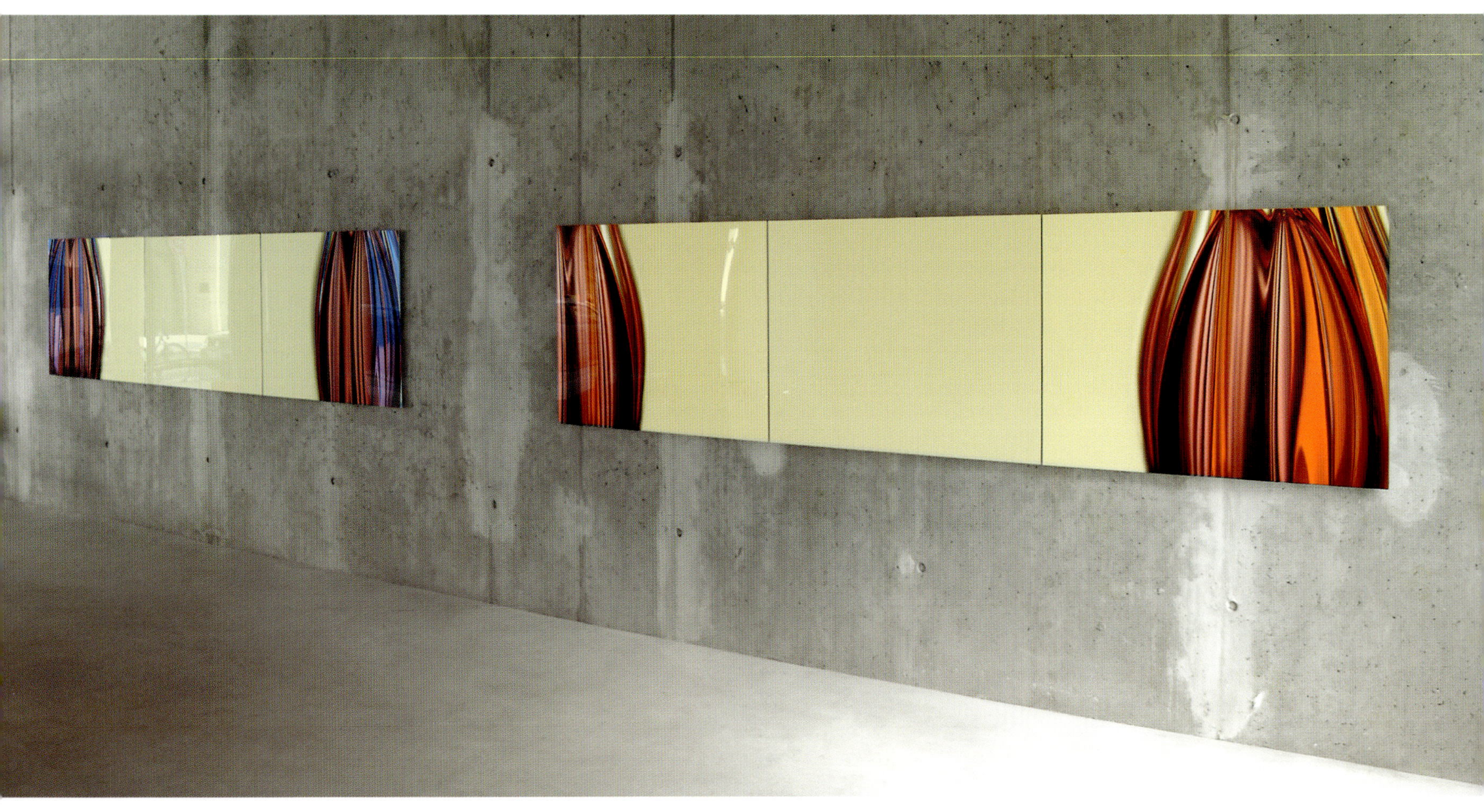

**Chromatic Plants** . 2006 . C-Print on Dibond with Diasec Face . Blue / Orange . Each 90 x 260 cm . BestregARTs . Frankfurt

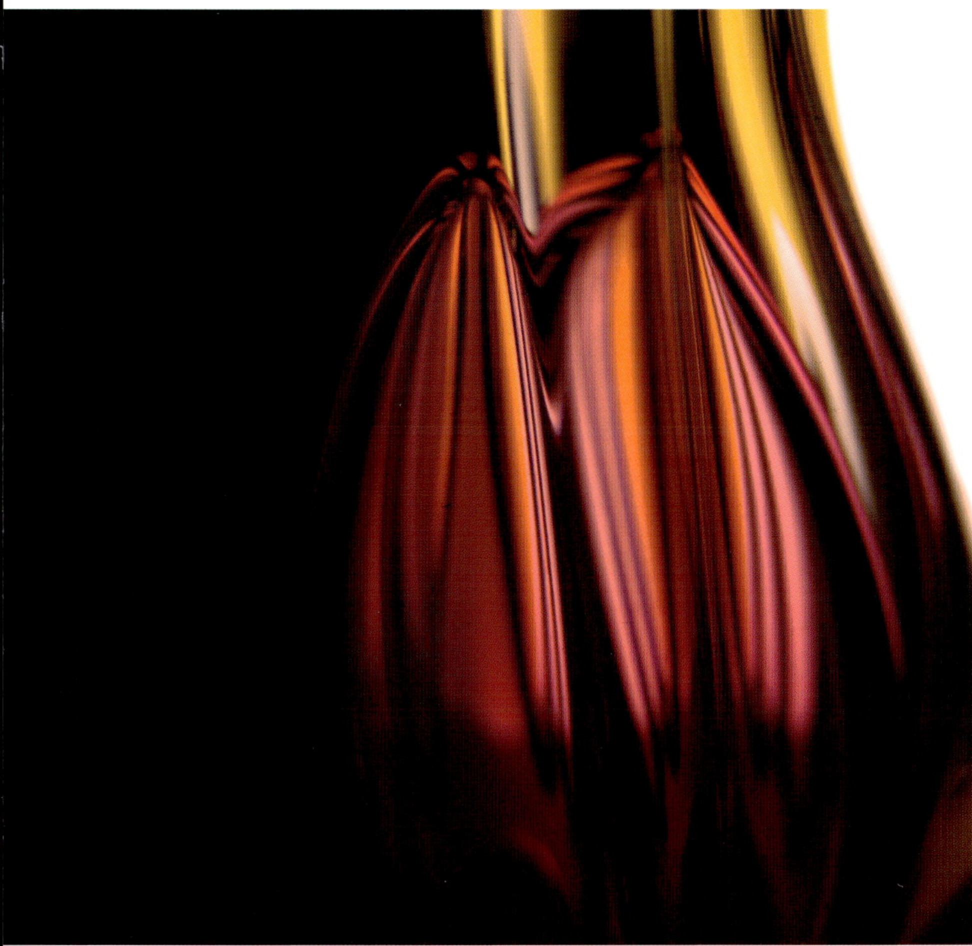



**Chromatic Plants** . 2006 . C-Print on Dibond with Diasec Face . Black . 115 x 125 cm . Gallery Bernd A. Lausberg . Düsseldorf

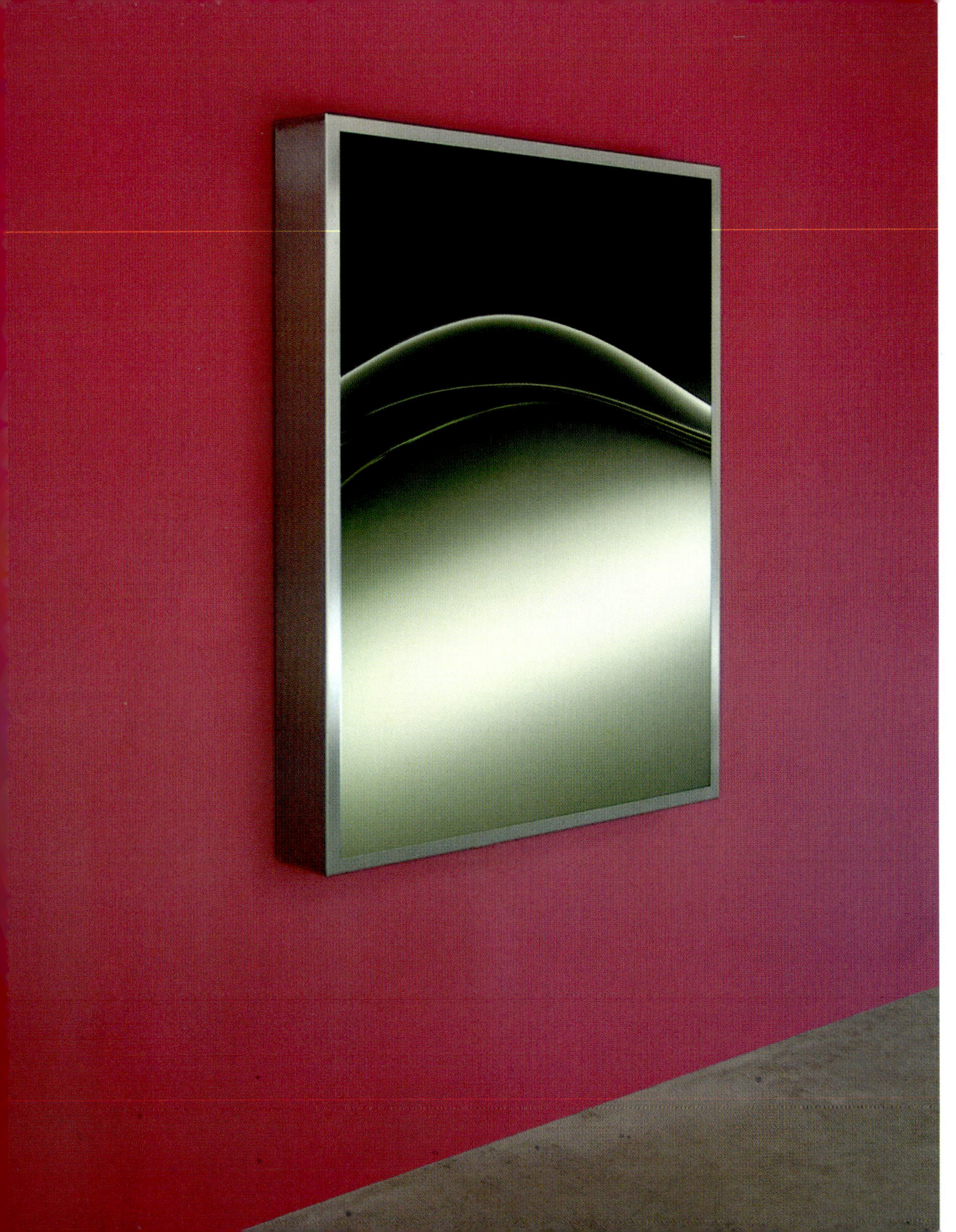

**Blade** . 2006
Stainless Steel Light Box . 135 x 104 x 15 cm
Luminale Frankfurt . 2006
[Patrick Heide Contemporary Art . BestregARTs]

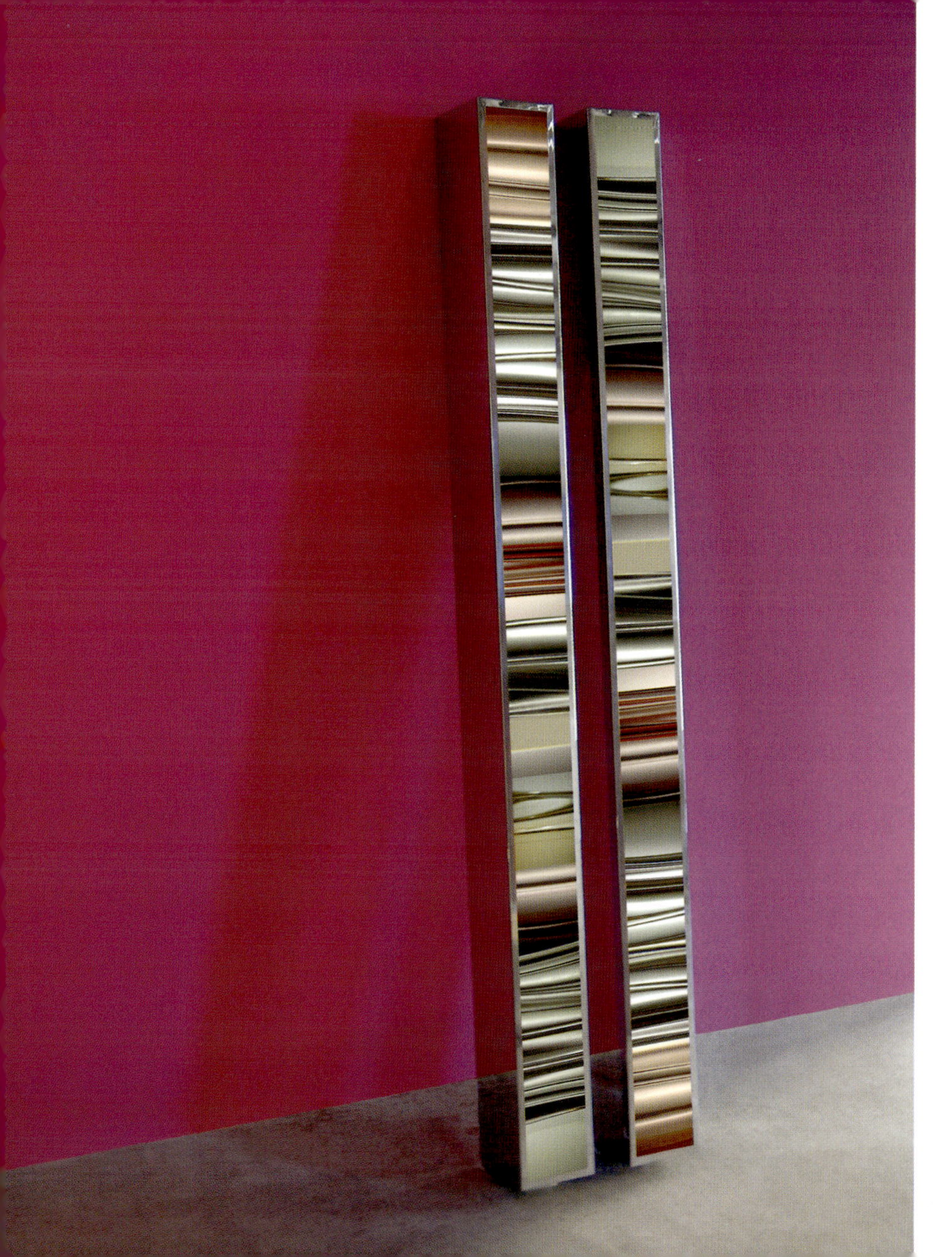

**Shades of Gray** . 2006
Chrome Light Boxes . Laserchrome Slide on Plexiglass . Each 188 x 15 x 15 cm
Luminale Frankfurt . 2006
[Patrick Heide Contemporary Art . BestregARTs]

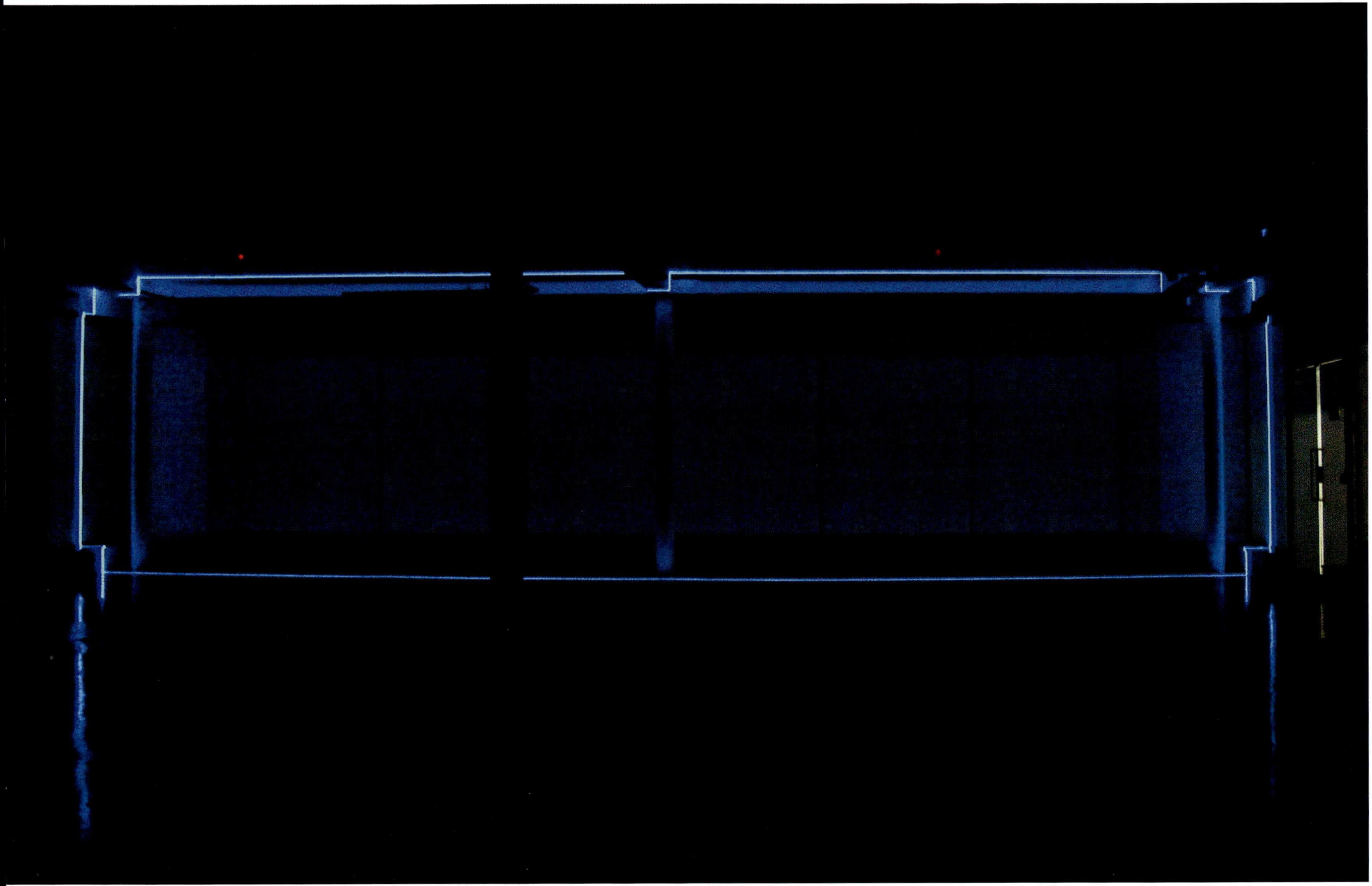

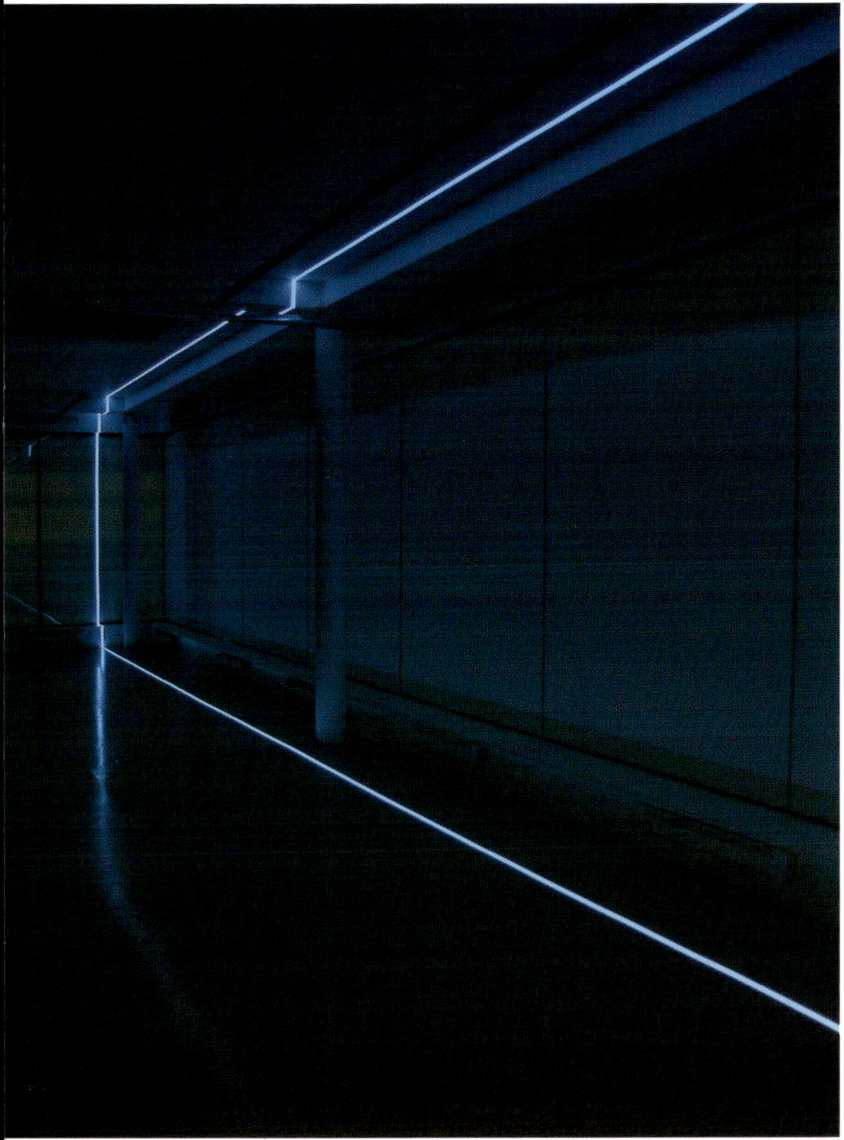

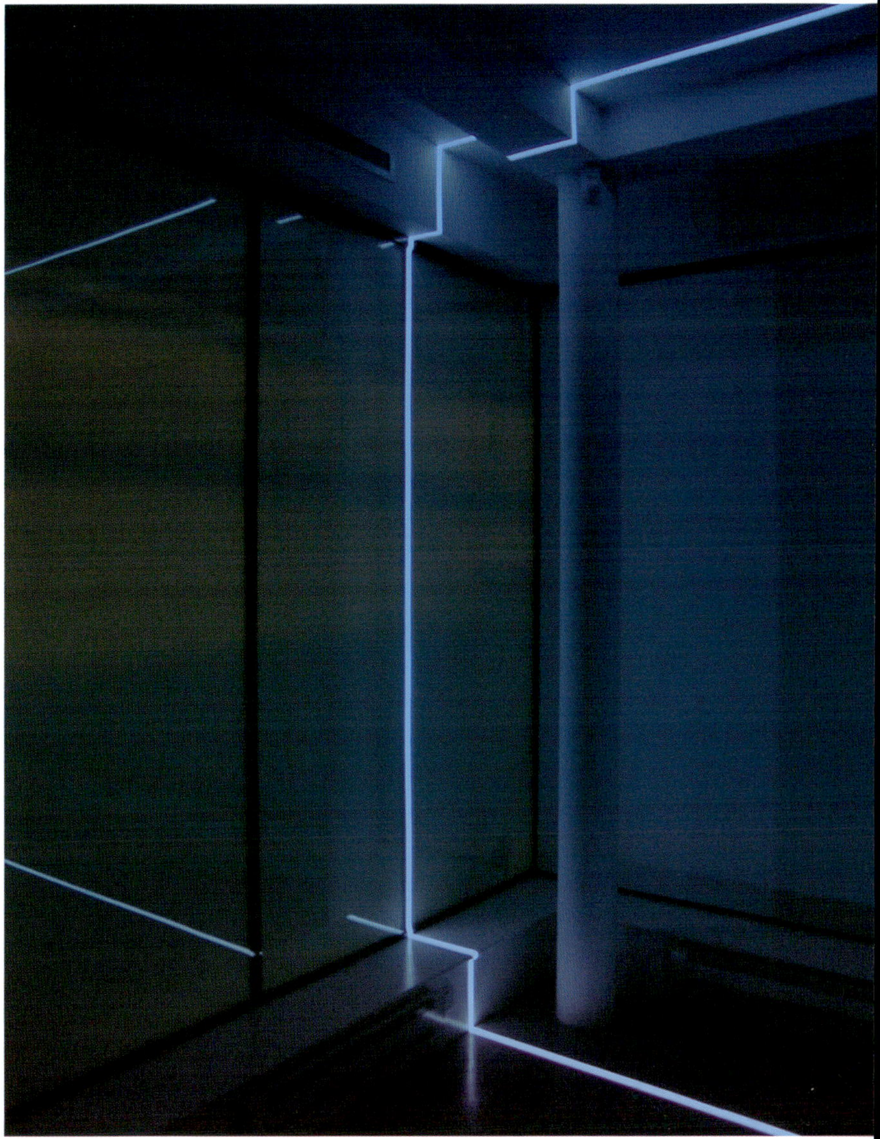

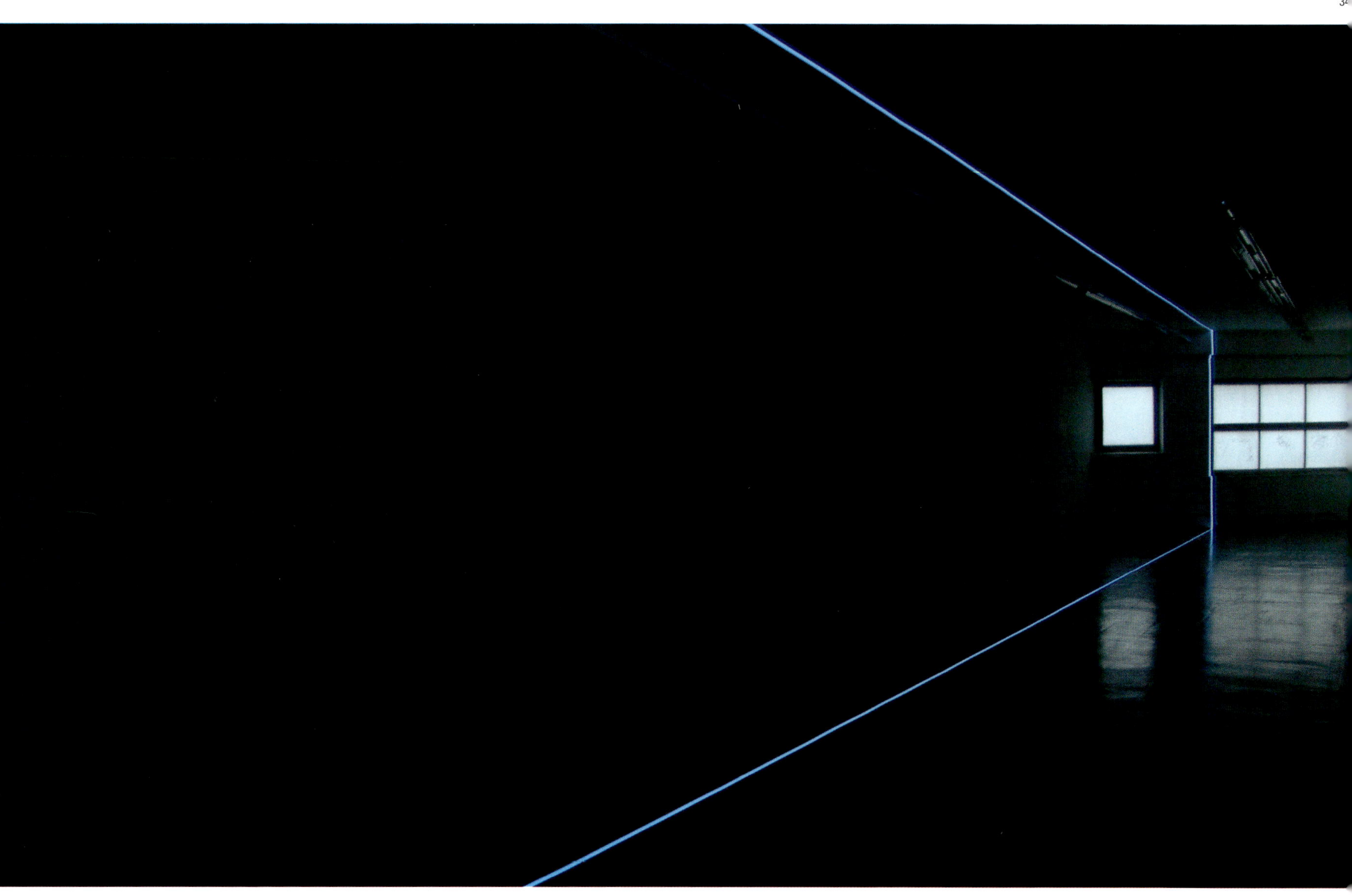

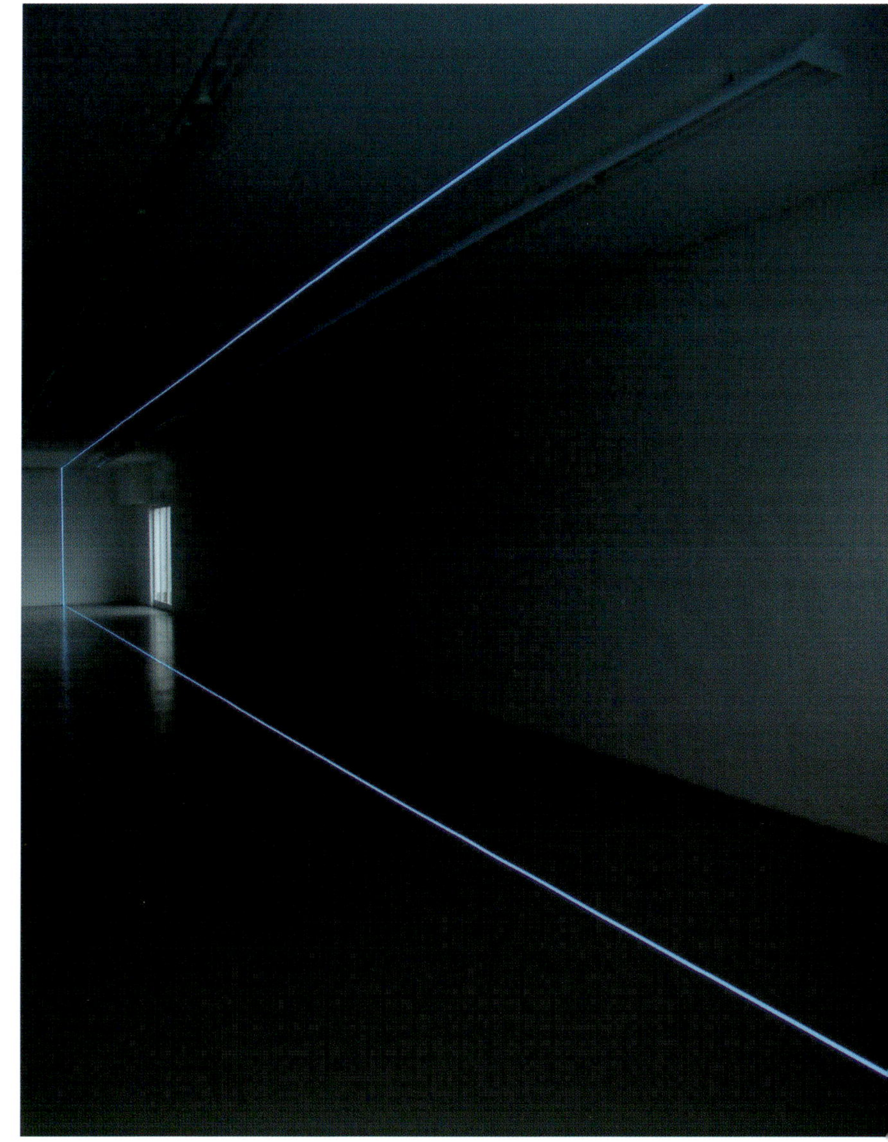

**Balance** . Electro Foil and Inverter
Dimension variable
2006 Kinetica Museum London [Permanent Collection]
2004 Kunstverein Ravensburg
2003 Kaiser Friedrich Berlin

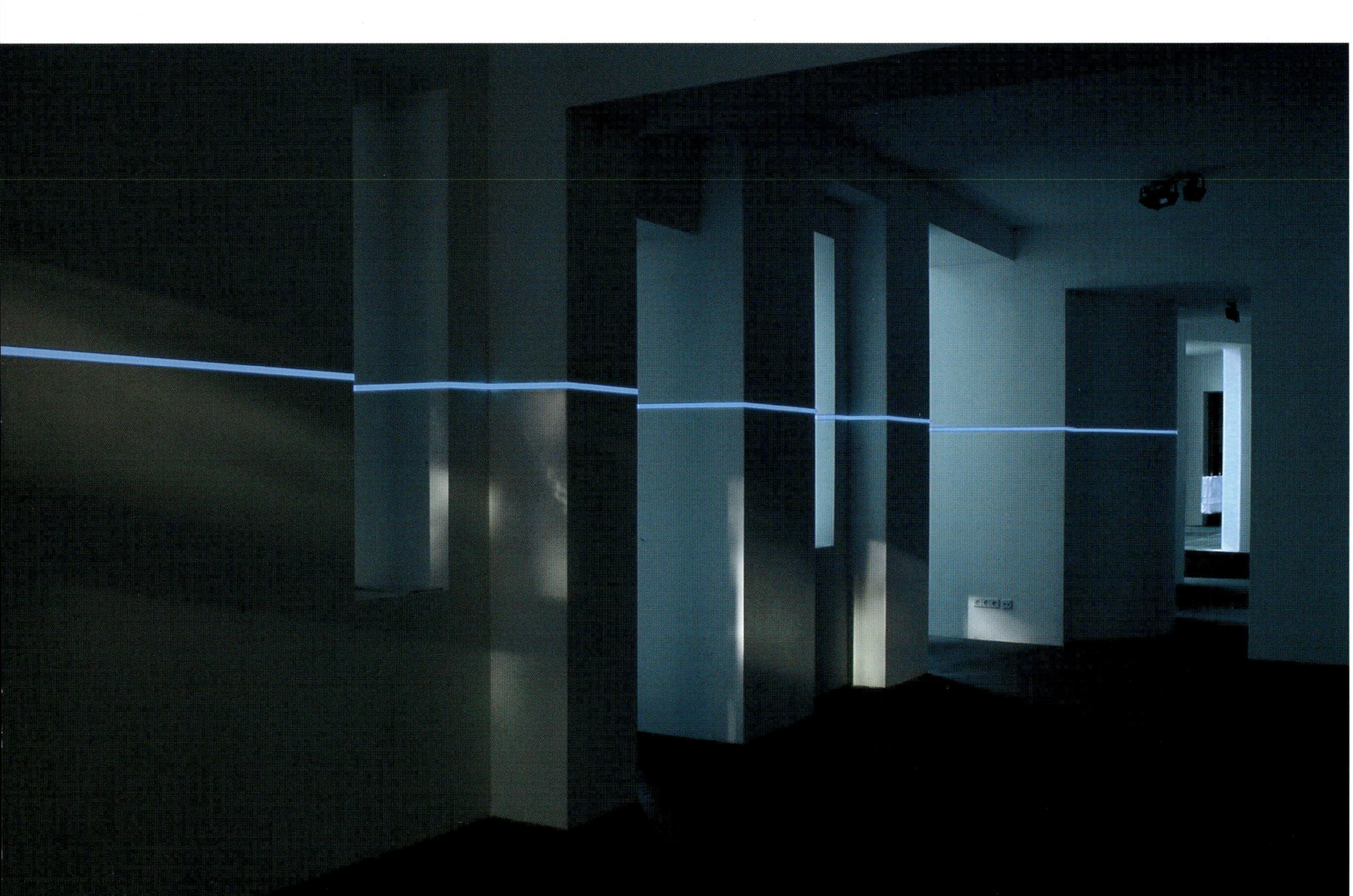

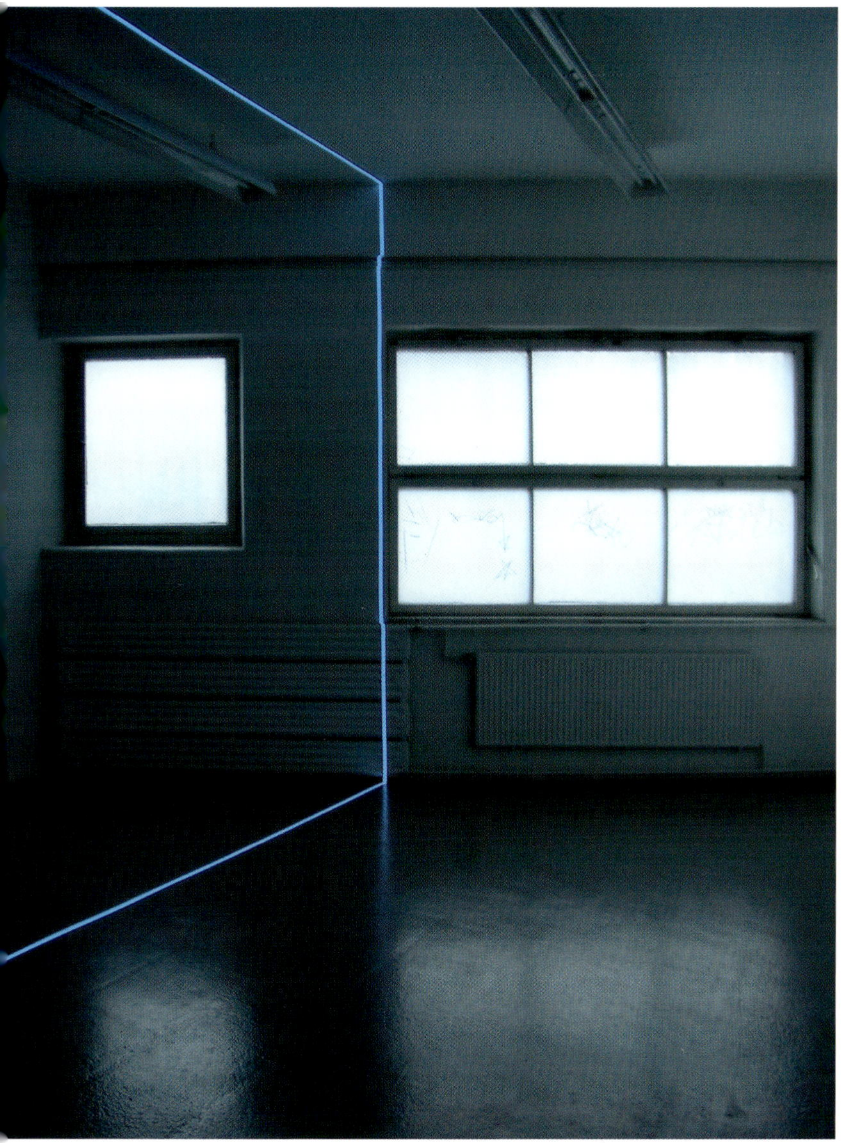

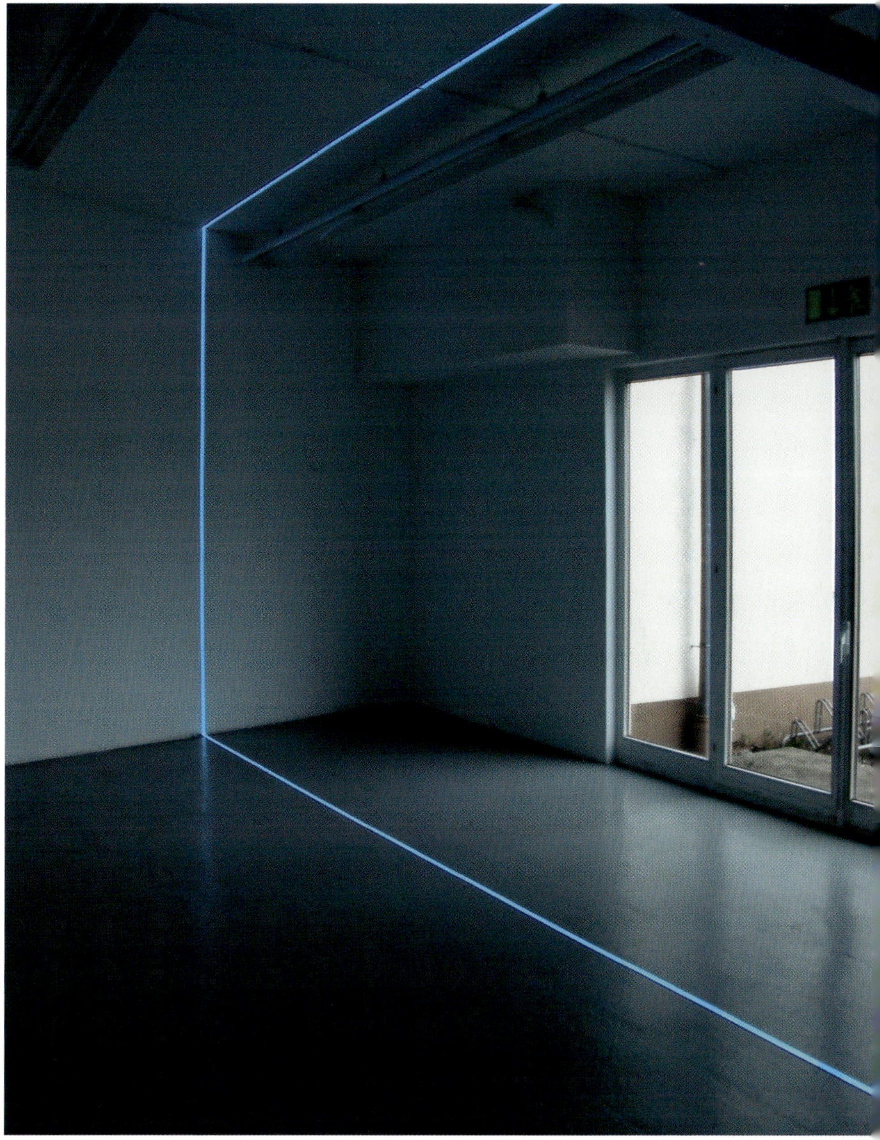

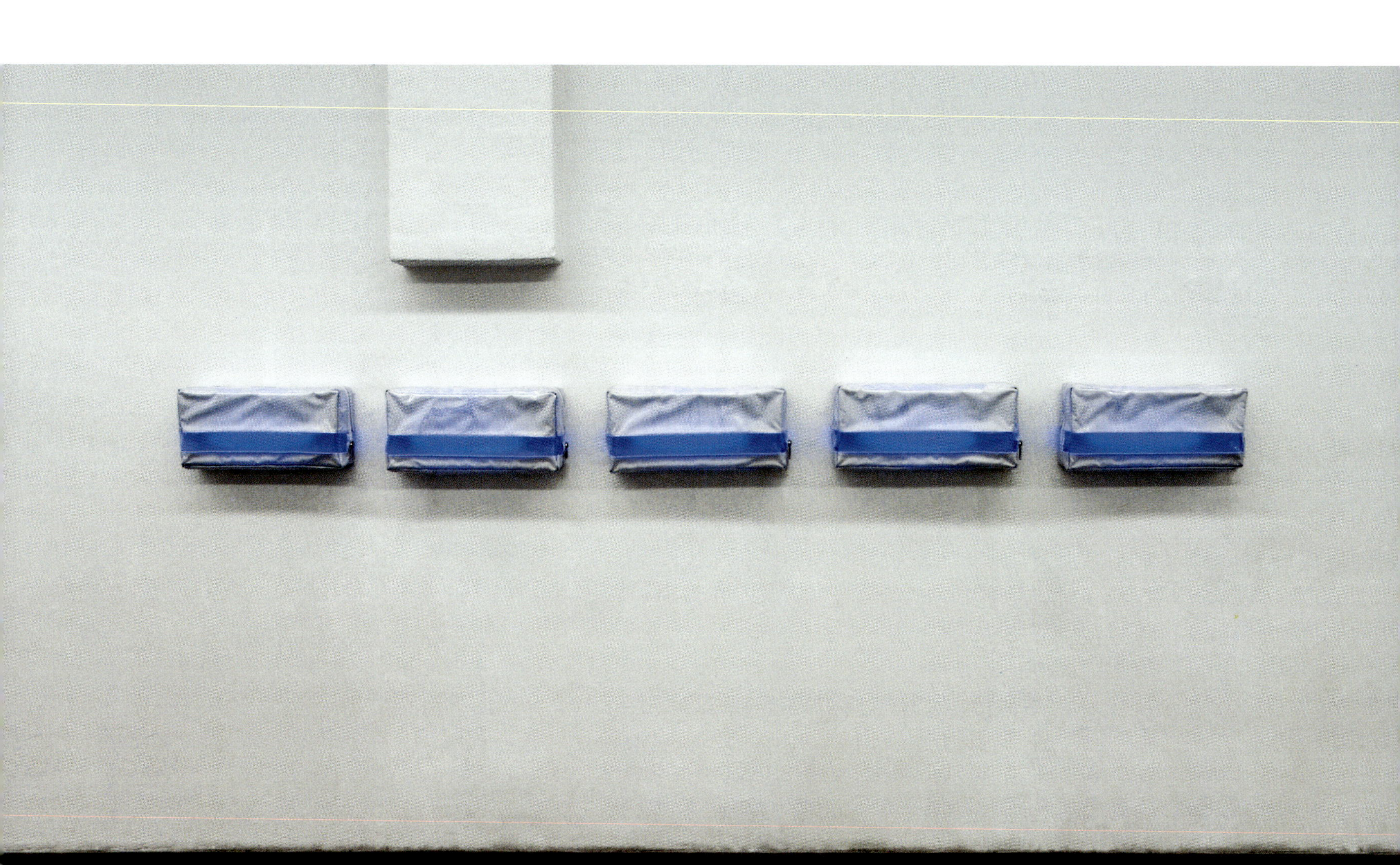

**Light in Plastic** . 2004 . 5 Light Boxes sewn from Tarpaulin . Neon . Plexiglass . Each 55 x 25 x 12 cm . Kunstverein Ravensburg

**Chromatic Impulse** . 2005 . LED Light Boxes . Each 42 x 42 x 2.5 cm . Berlinische Galerie with Spectral

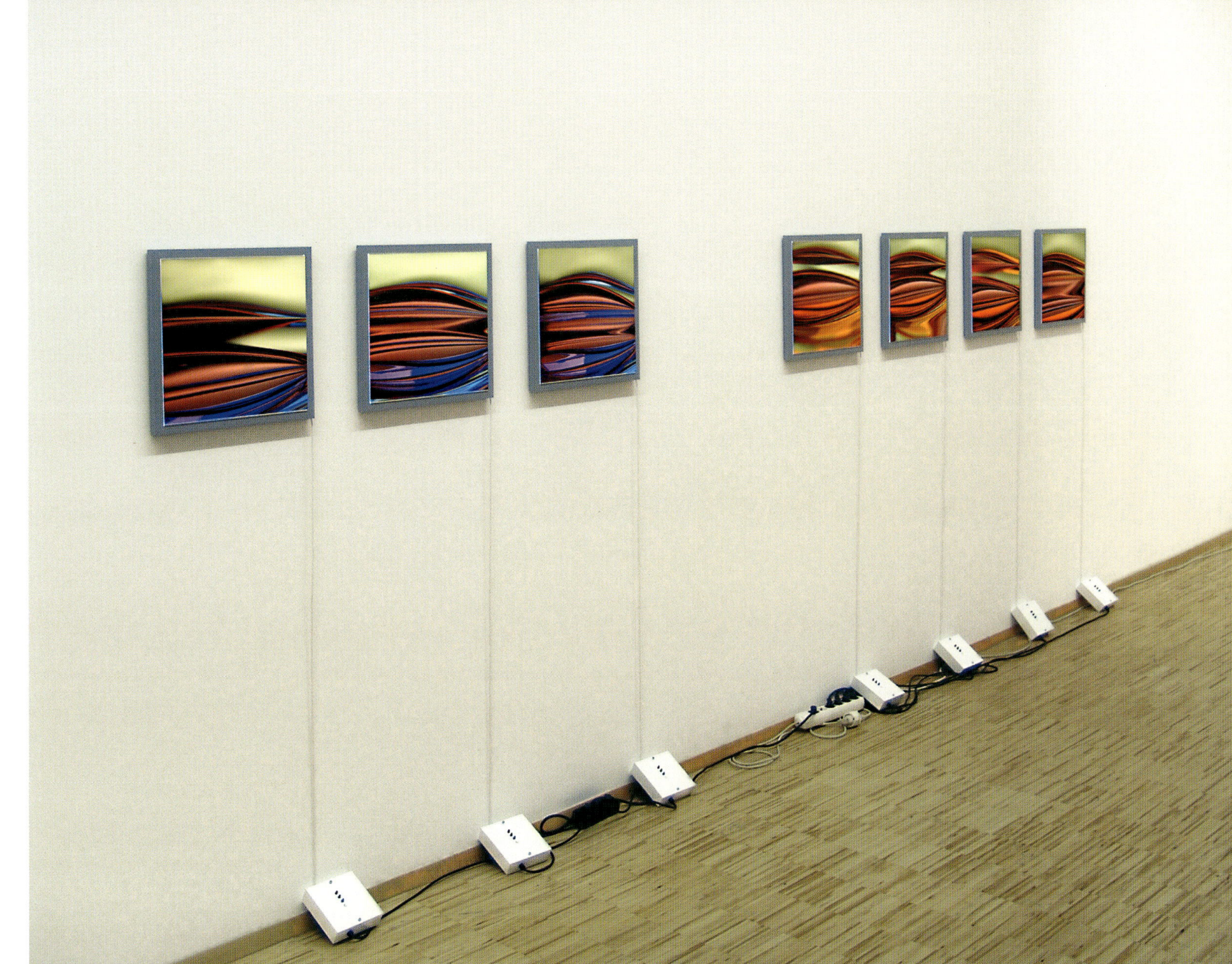

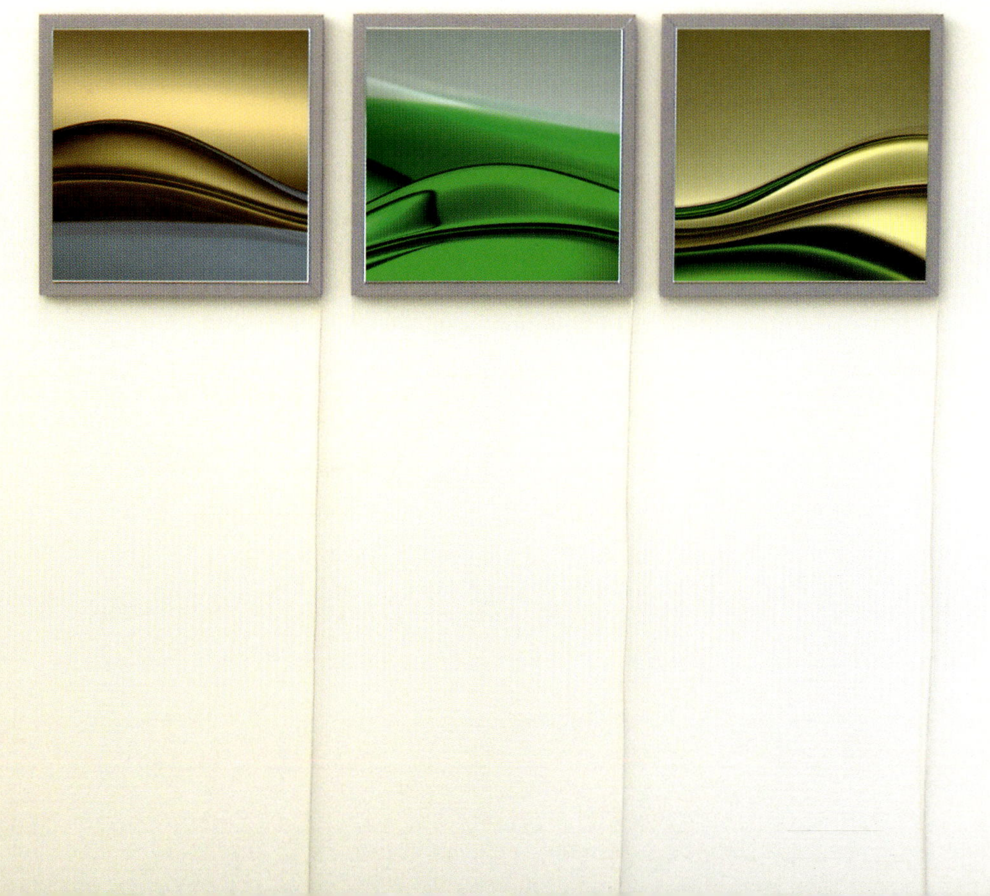

**Chromatic Impulse** . 2006
LED Light Boxes
Each 42 x 42 x 2.5 cm
[Lufthansa Frankfurt]

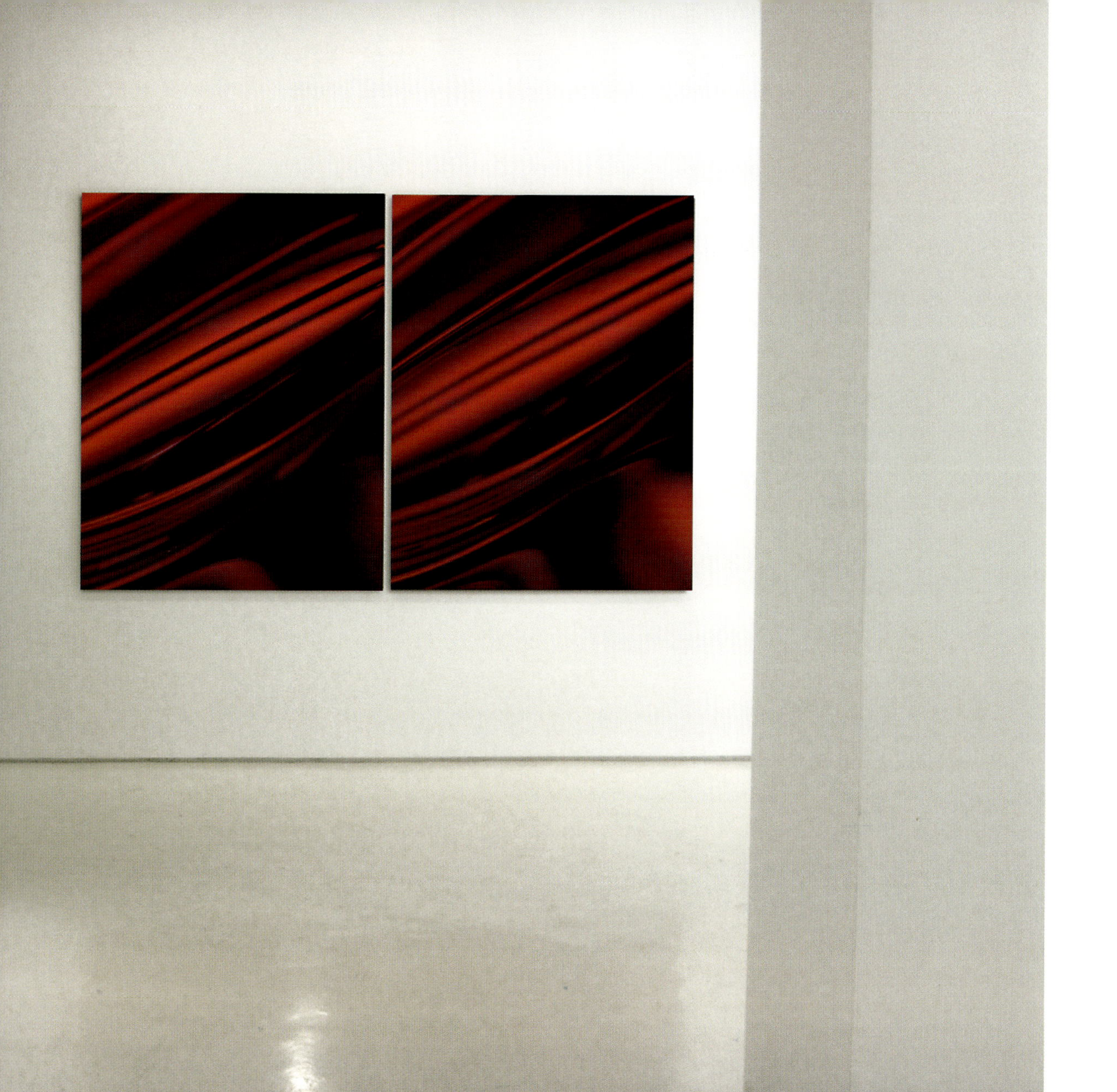

**Red** . 2005
C-Print on Dibond with Diasec Face
Edition 3+1 . 160 x 240 cm
Gallery Kashya Hildebrand . New York

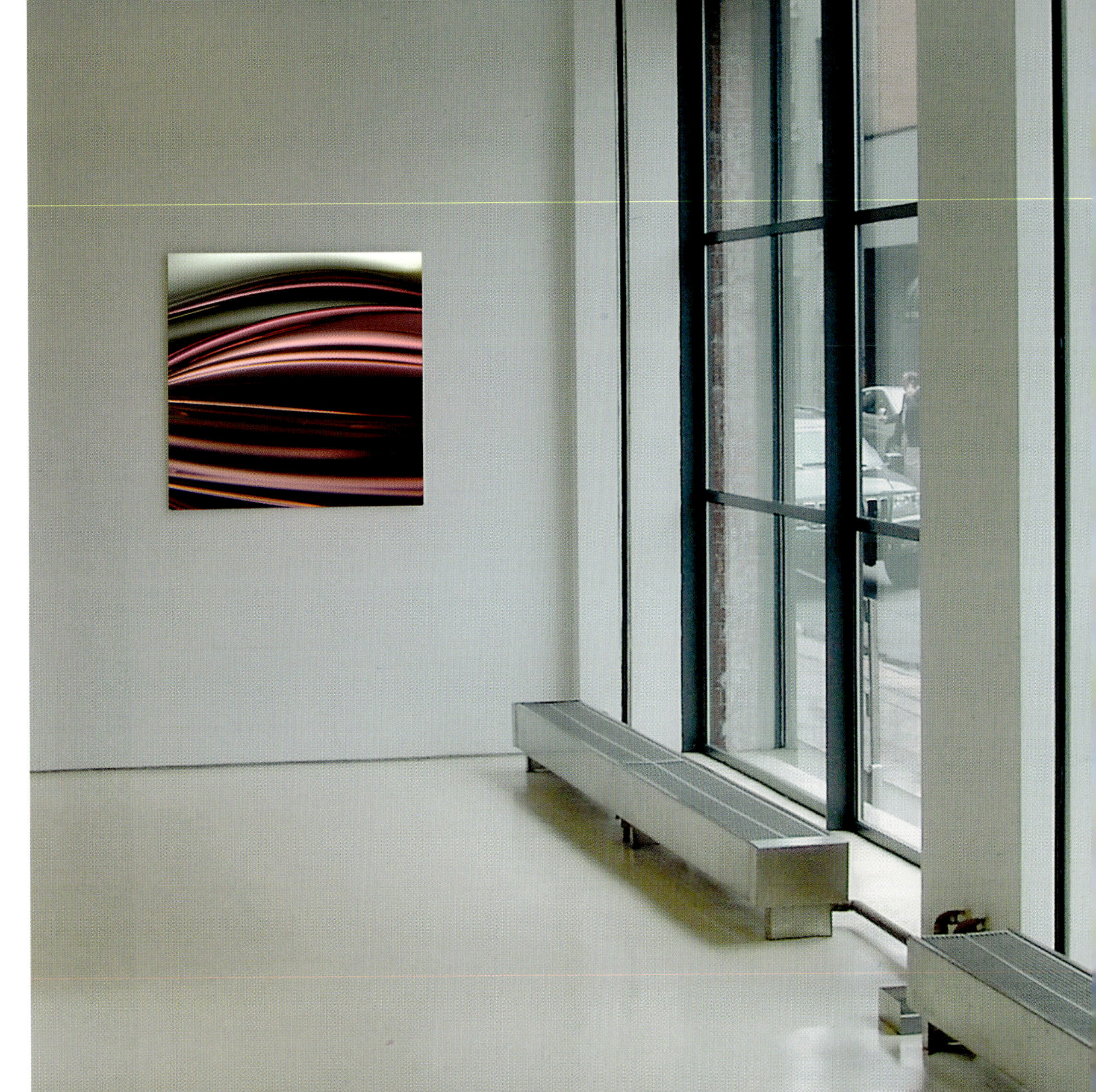

**Transmutation Magenta** . 2005
C-Print on Dibond with Diasec Face
Edition 3+1 . 100 x 100 cm
[Collection of the German Parliament]

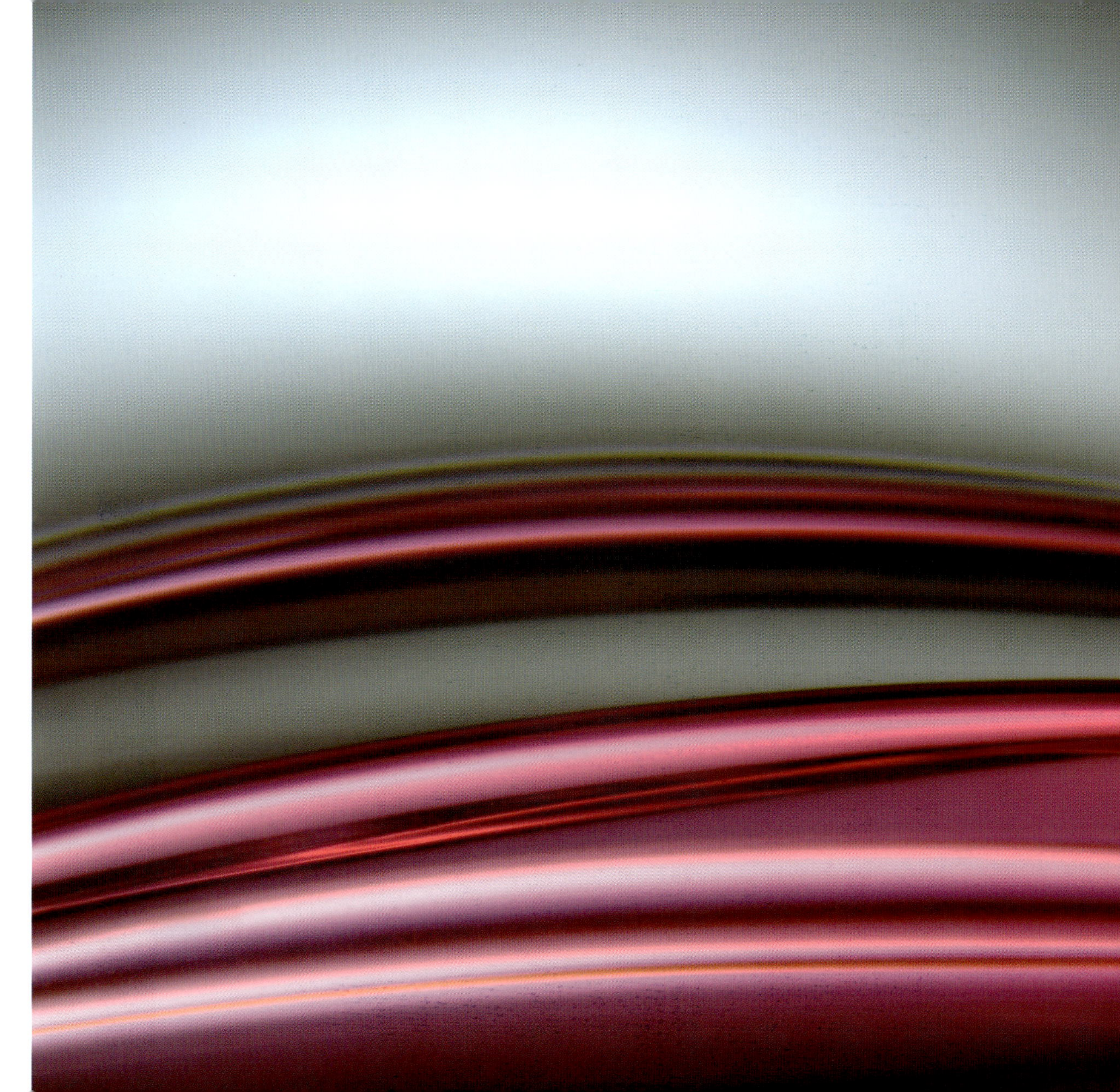

**Chromatic Impulse** . 2007
LED Light Box . 120 x 120 x 2 cm
[Targetti Light Art Collection]

Illumination . 2004 . 8 Light Boxes sewn from Tarpaulin . Neon . Plexiglass . Blue Glass Frits . Each 155 x 55 x 15 cm . Aedes Berlin

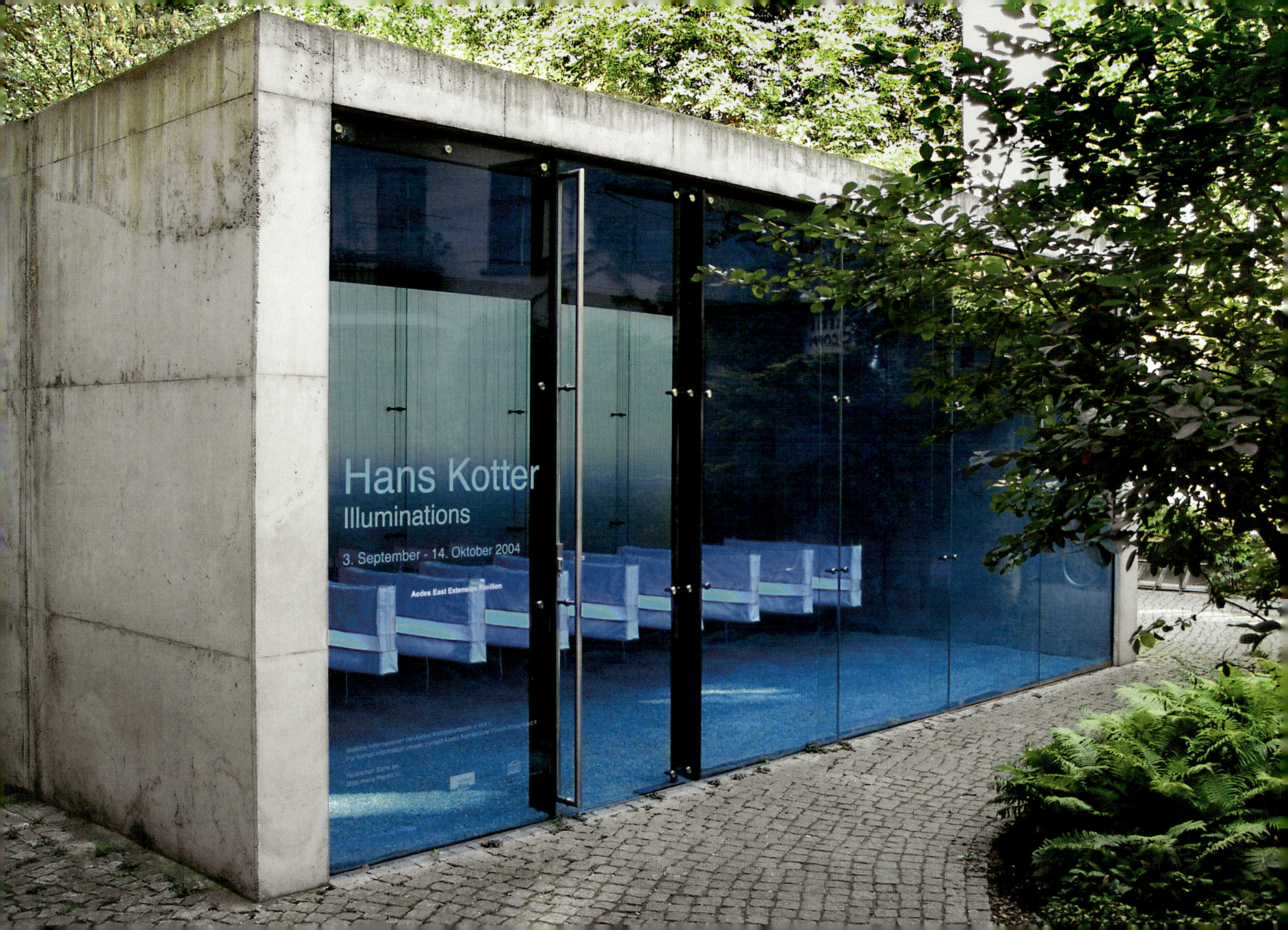

Hans Kotter
Illuminations
3. September - 14. Oktober 2004
Aedes East Extension Pavillon

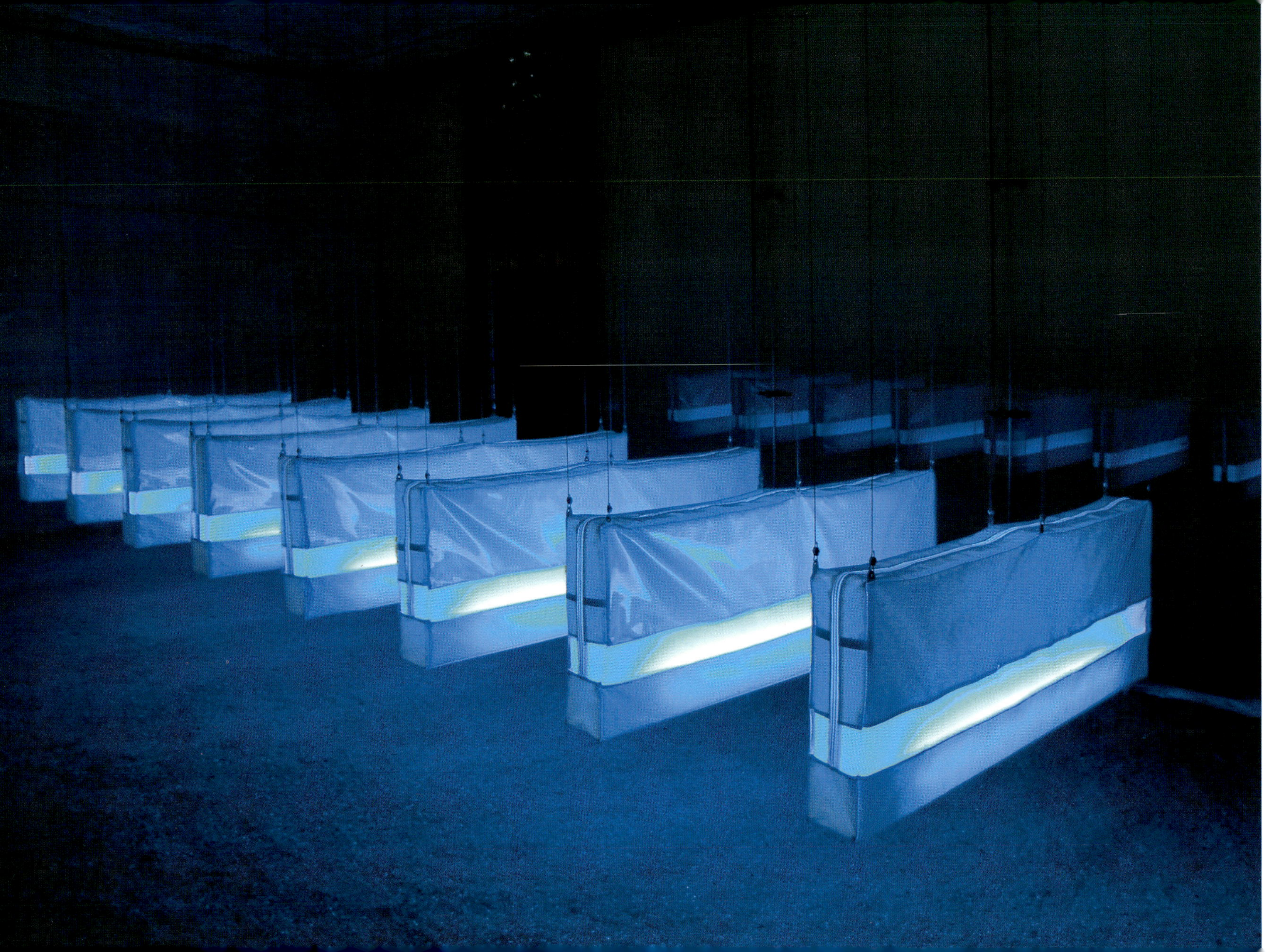

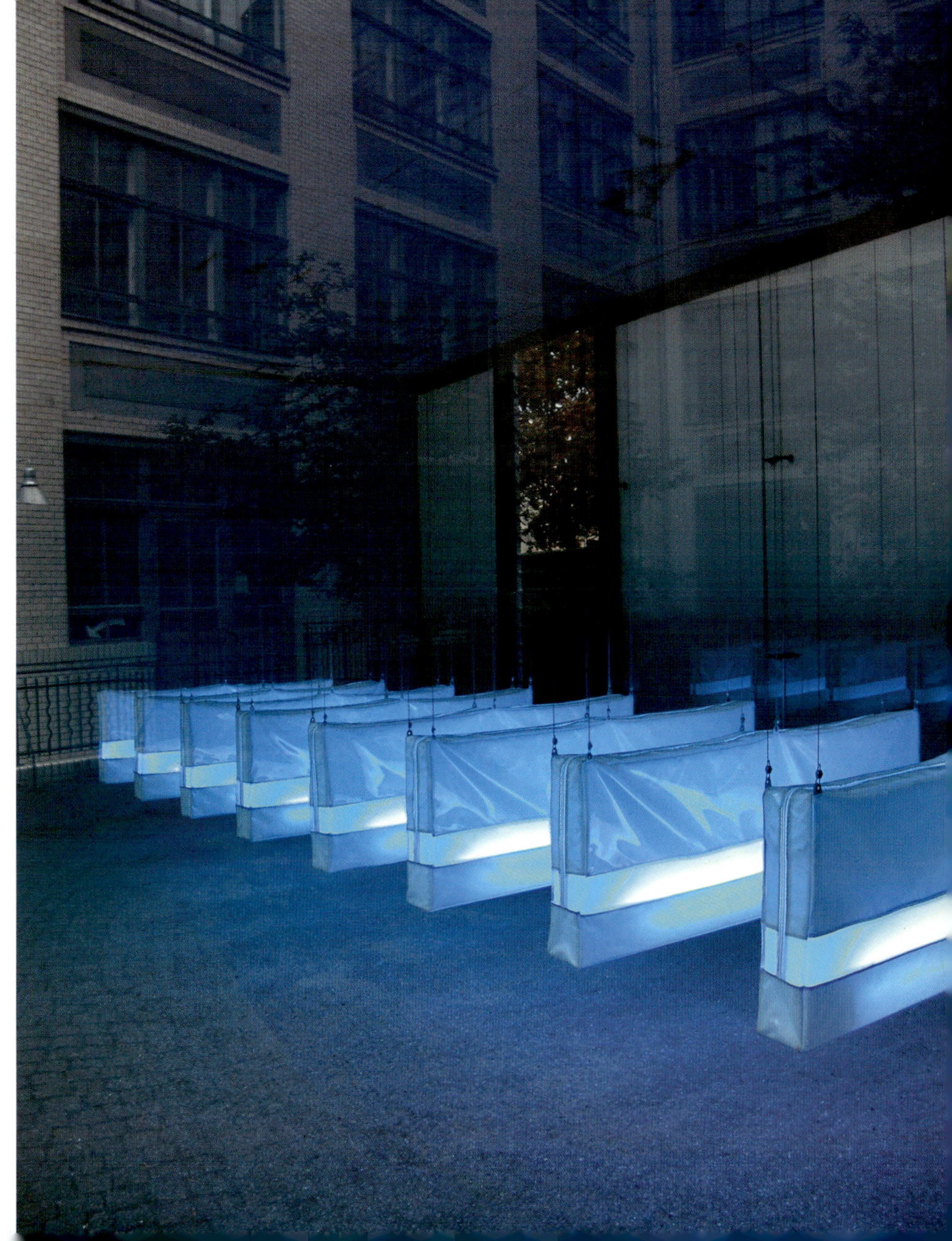

**TV Shot** . 2003 . Light Boxes sewn from Tarpaulin . Slide . Neon . Plexiglass . 110 x 150 cm . Lightfast . Patrick Heide Contemporary Art . Frankfurt

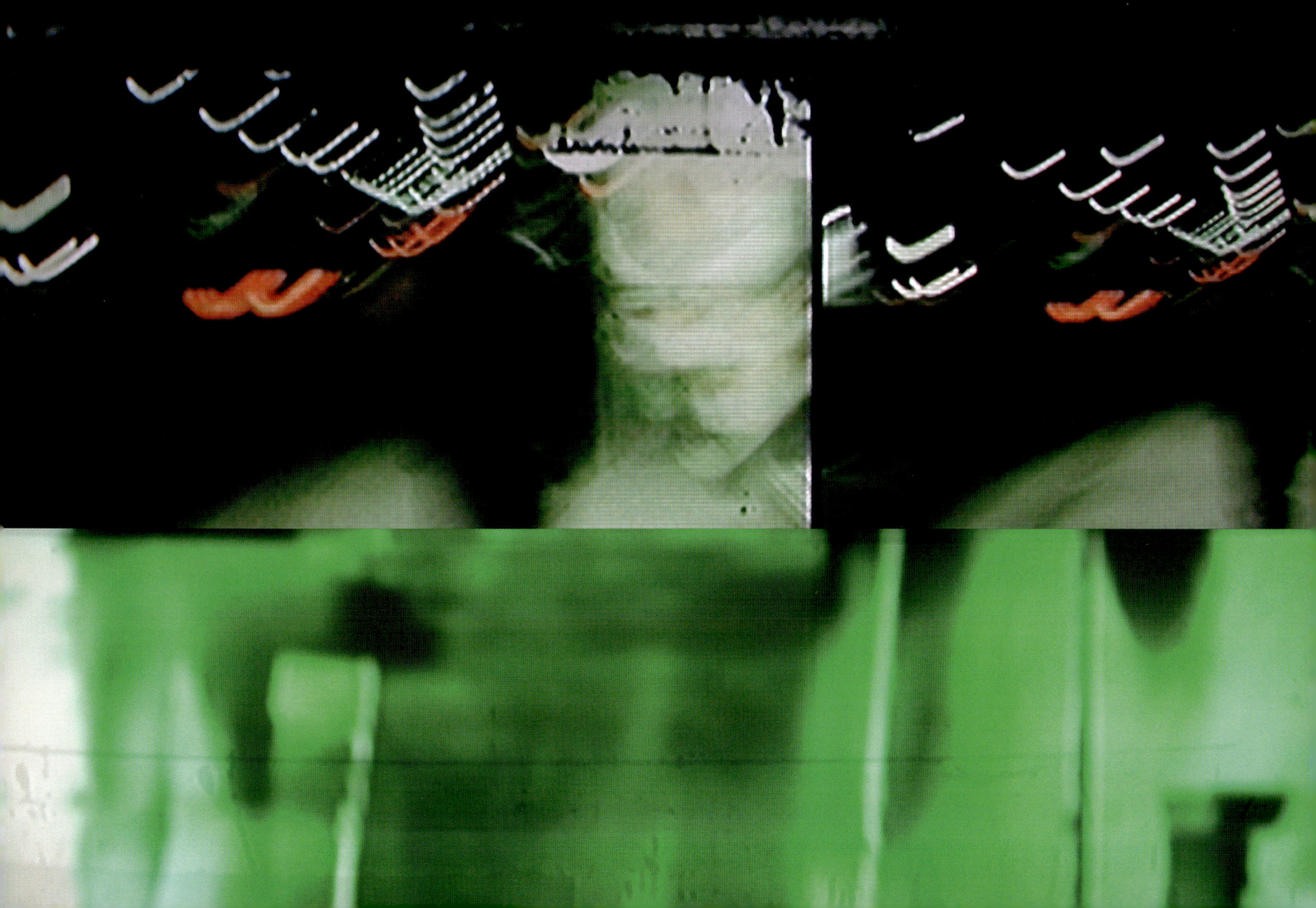

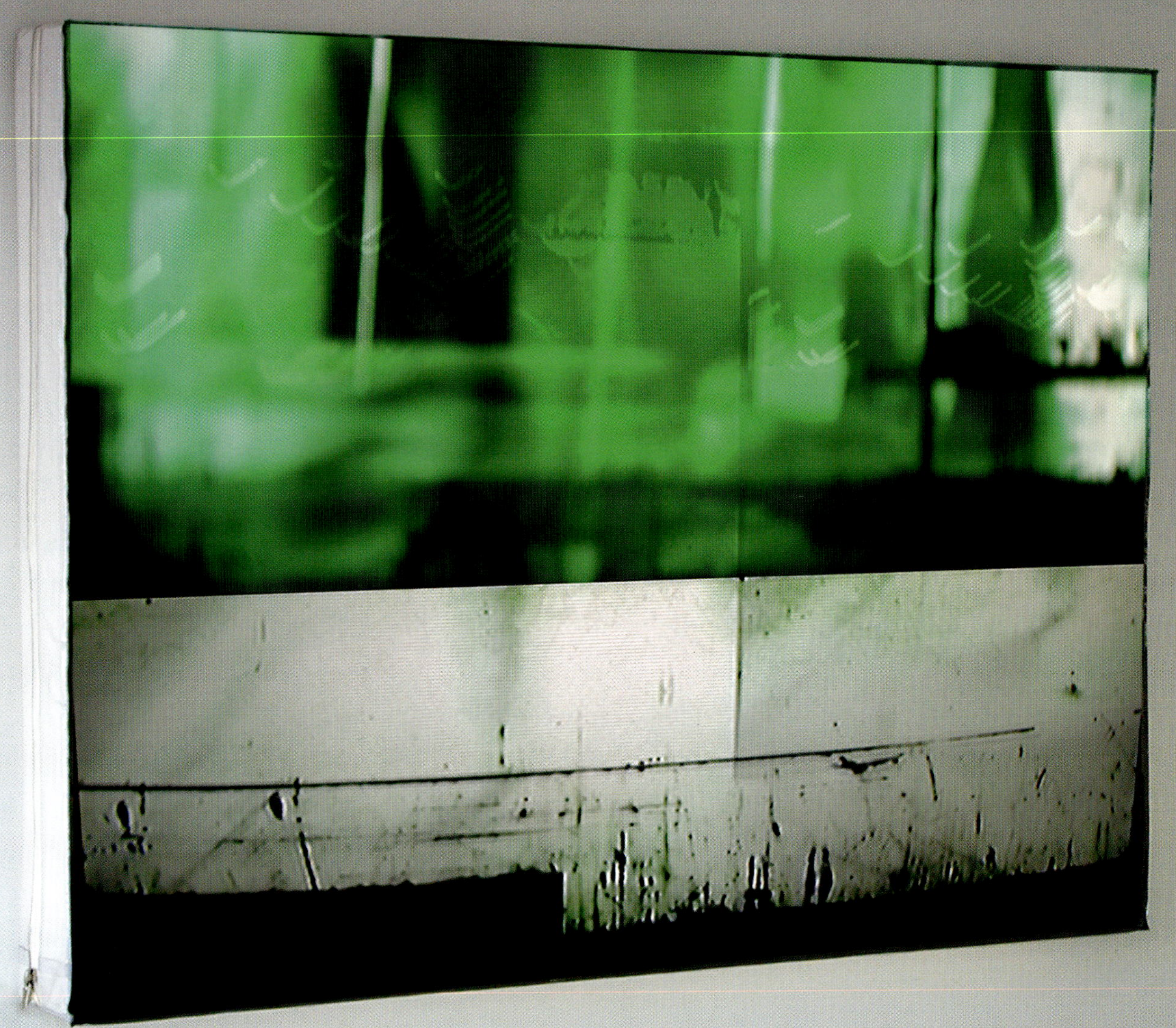

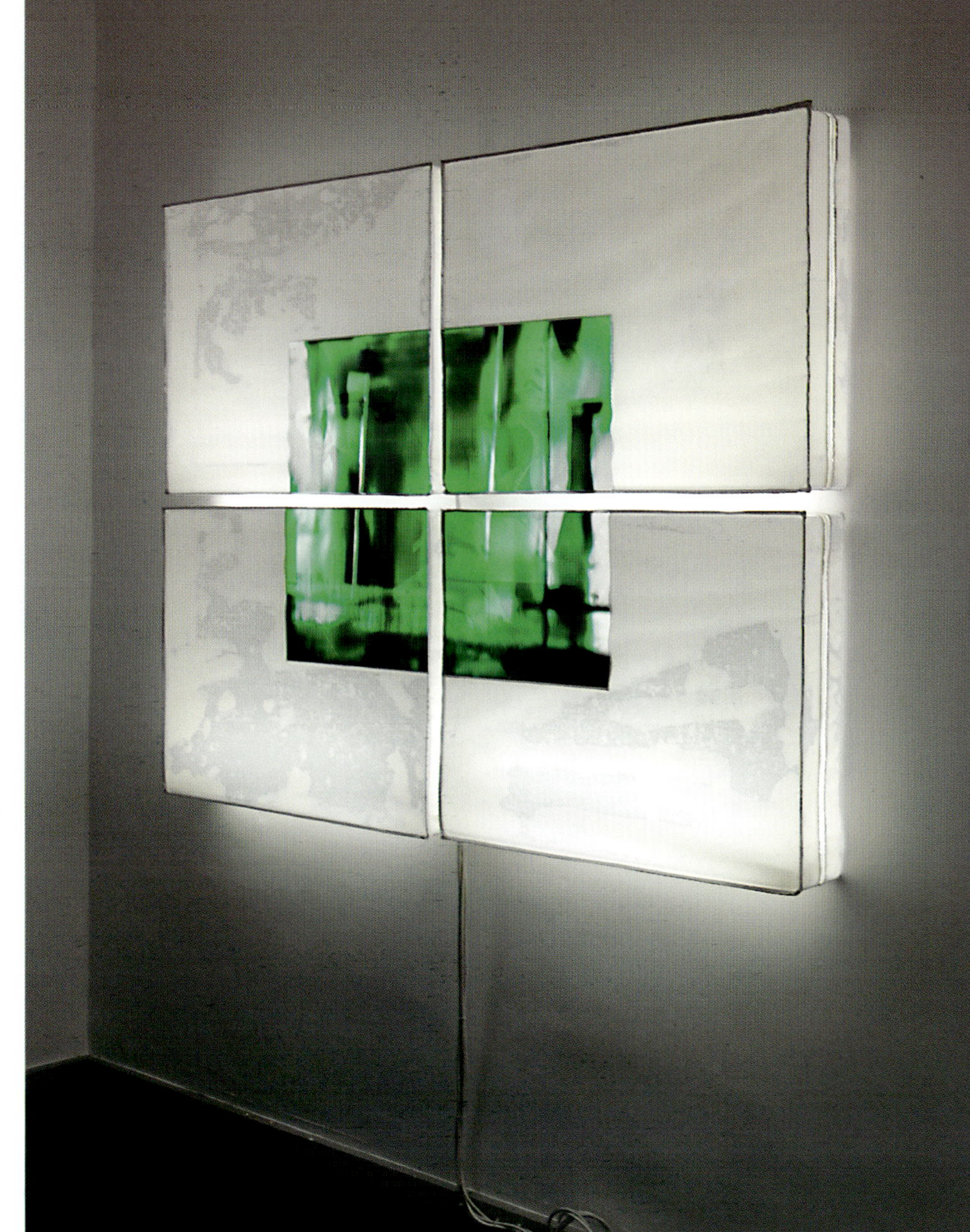

**TV Shot** . 2003 . Light Boxes sewn from Tarpaulin Slide
Neon . Plexiglass . 123 x 165 cm
Lightfast . Patrick Heide Contemporary Art . Frankfurt

**TV Shot** . 2003 . Light Boxes sewn from Tarpaulin Slide
Neon . Plexiglass . 165 x 205 cm
Lightfast . Patrick Heide Contemporary Art . Frankfurt

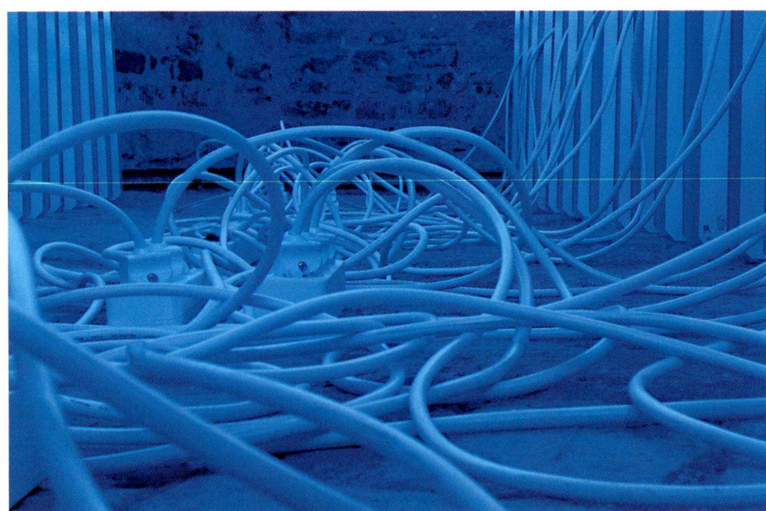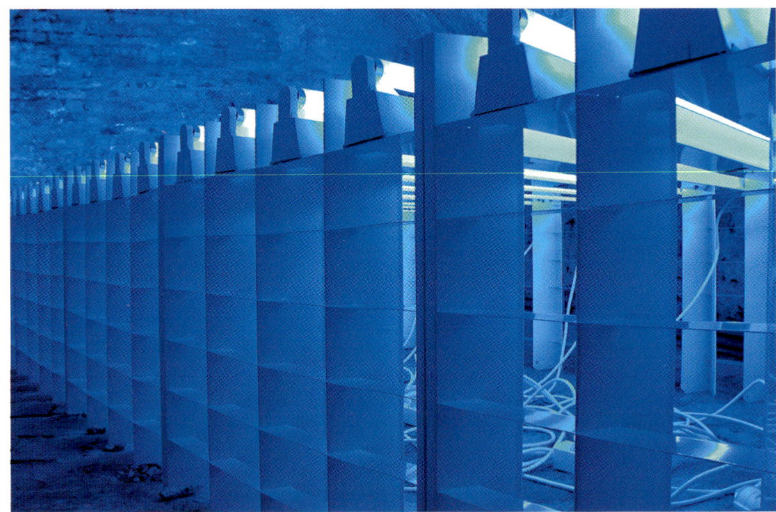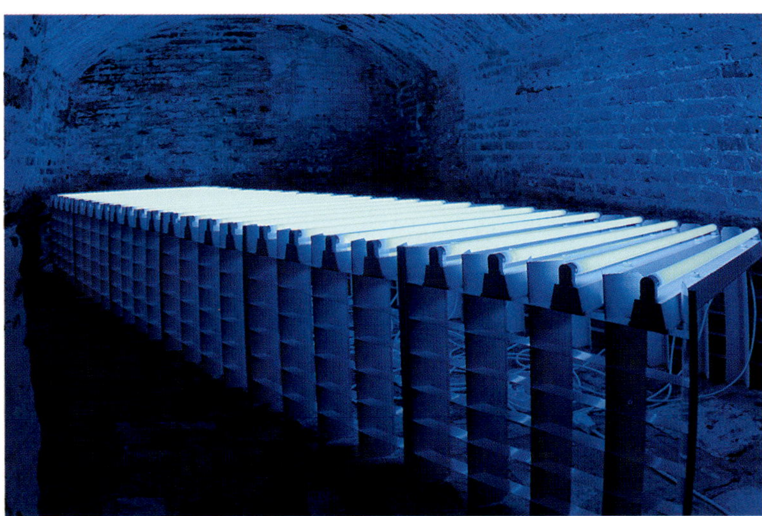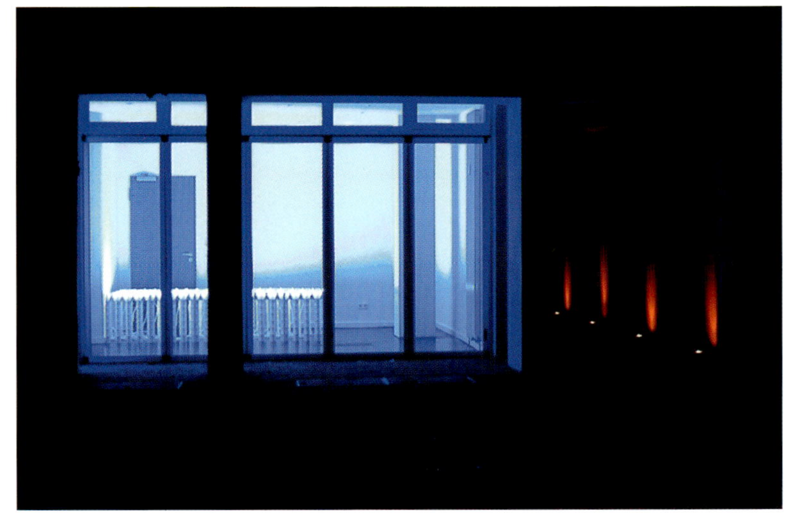

**Folding Bed** . Metal . Neon . 122 x 357 x 55 cm . 2003 Schloß Hohenschönhausen . 2003 Kaiser Friedrich Berlin . 2002 Galerie Bezirk Oberbayern . Munich . 2002 Stadtmuseum Neuötting

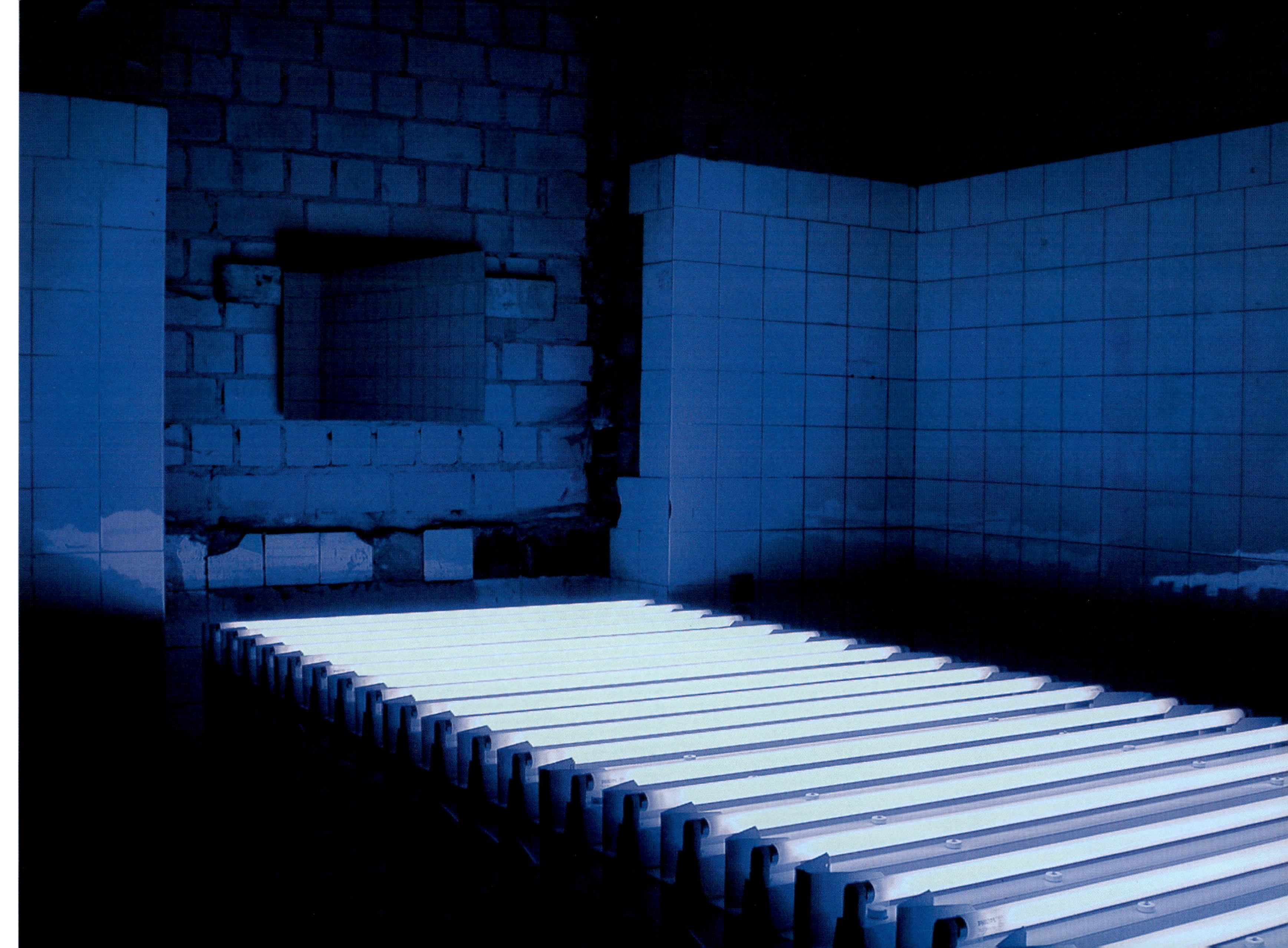

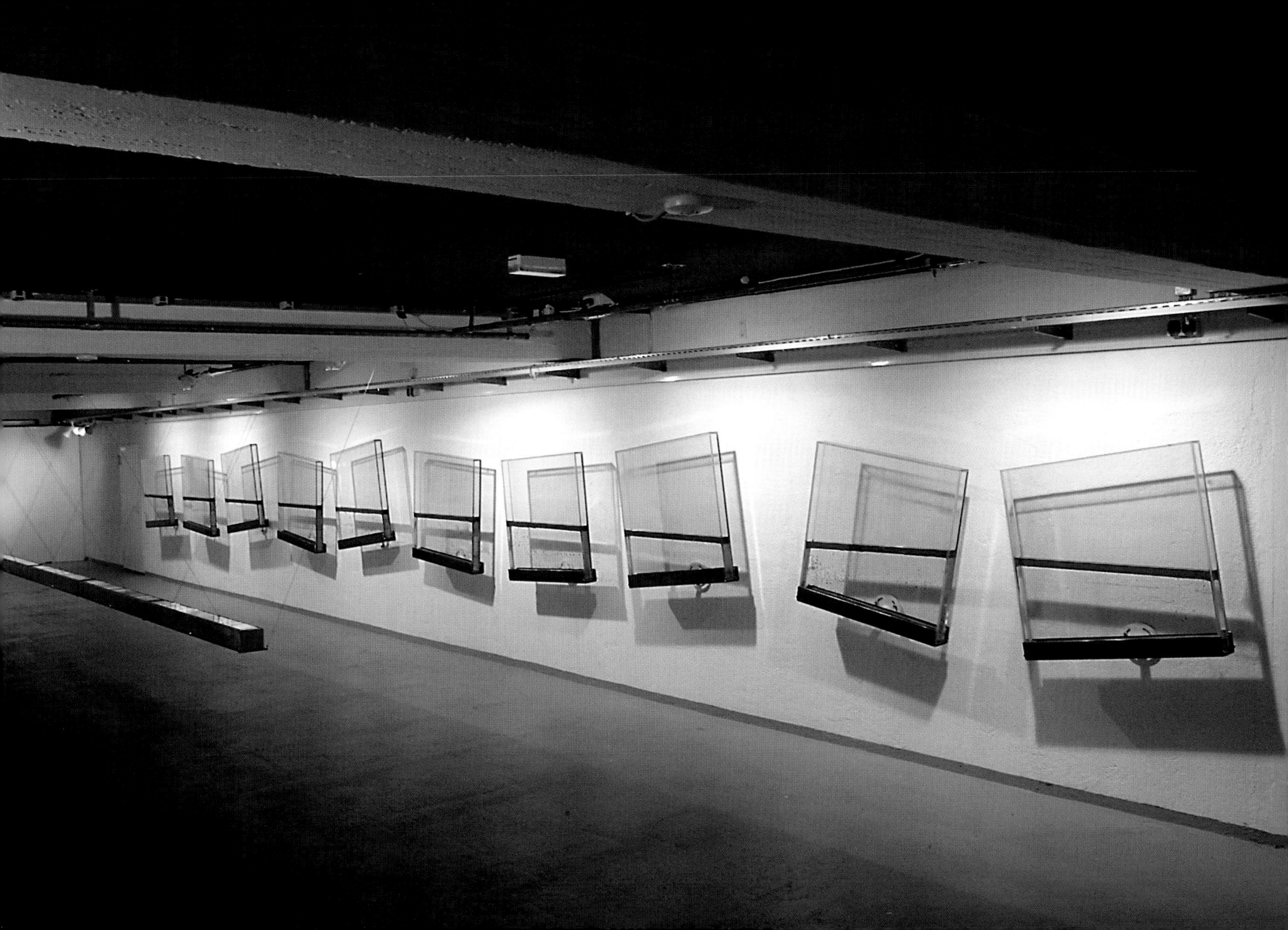

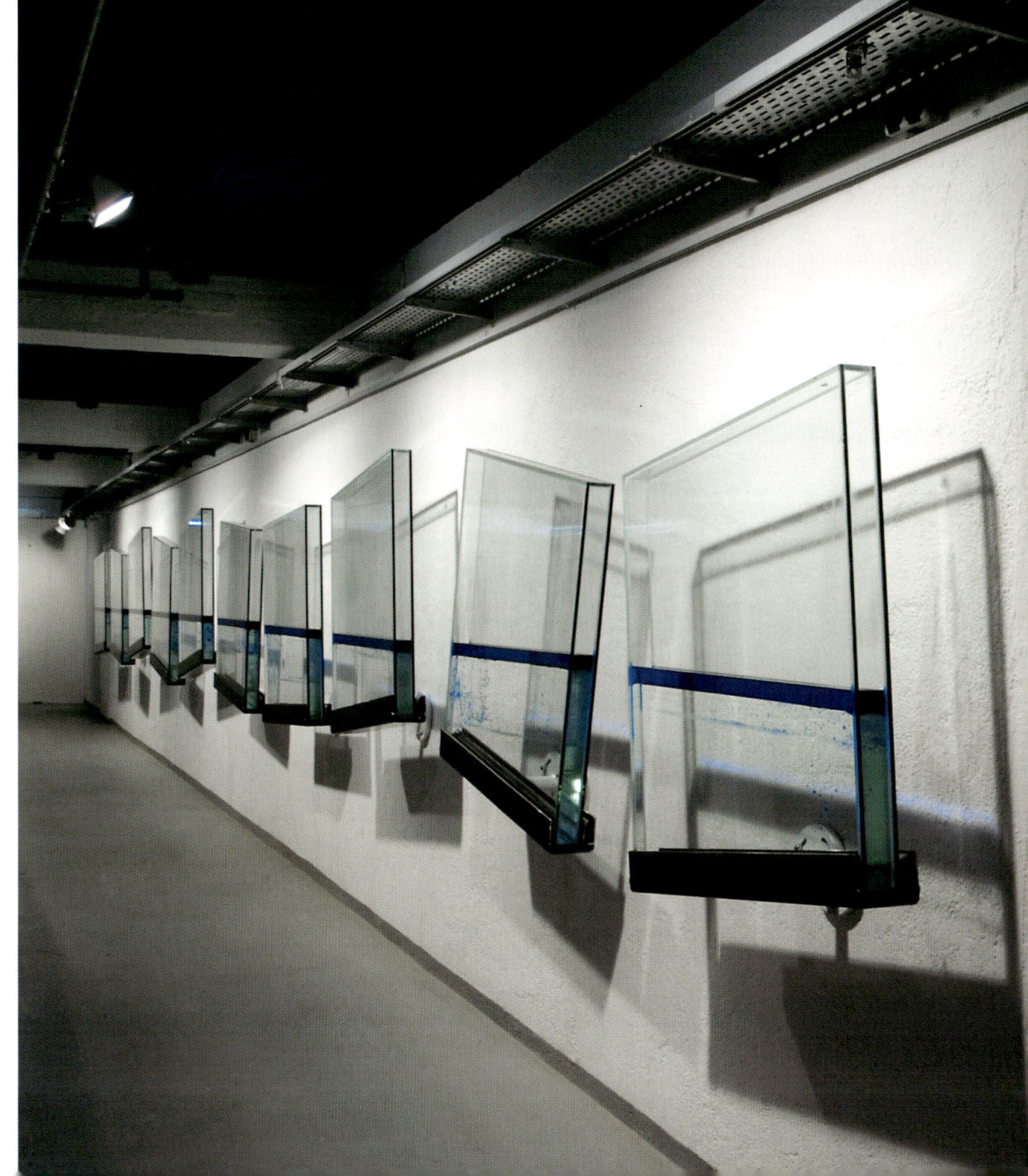



**Blue Line** . 2001
Glass . Blue Silicon Oil . Water . Metal
Each 100 x 100 cm
Pasinger Fabrik . Munich

School in Bavaria . Germany . 2007

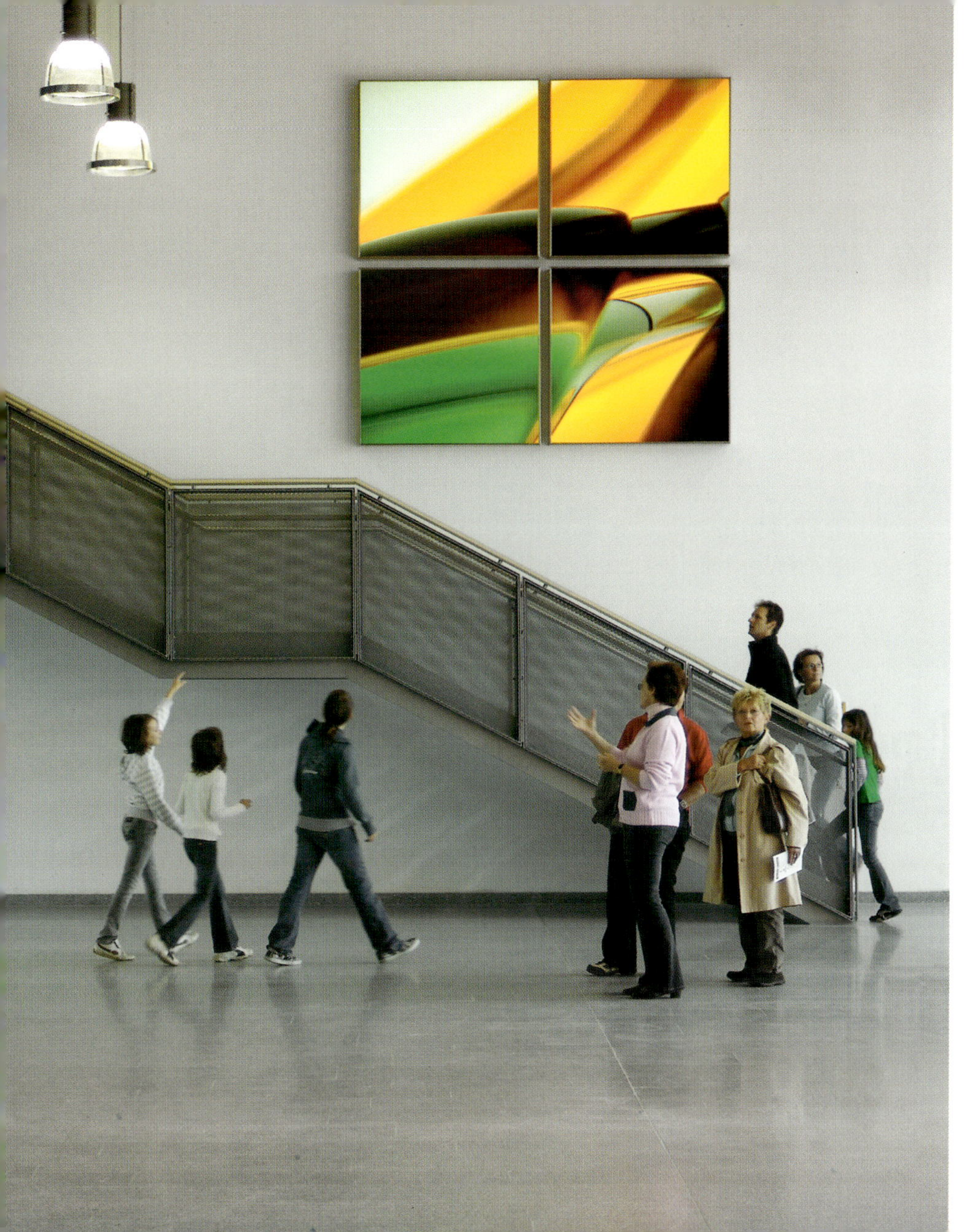

# Public Art

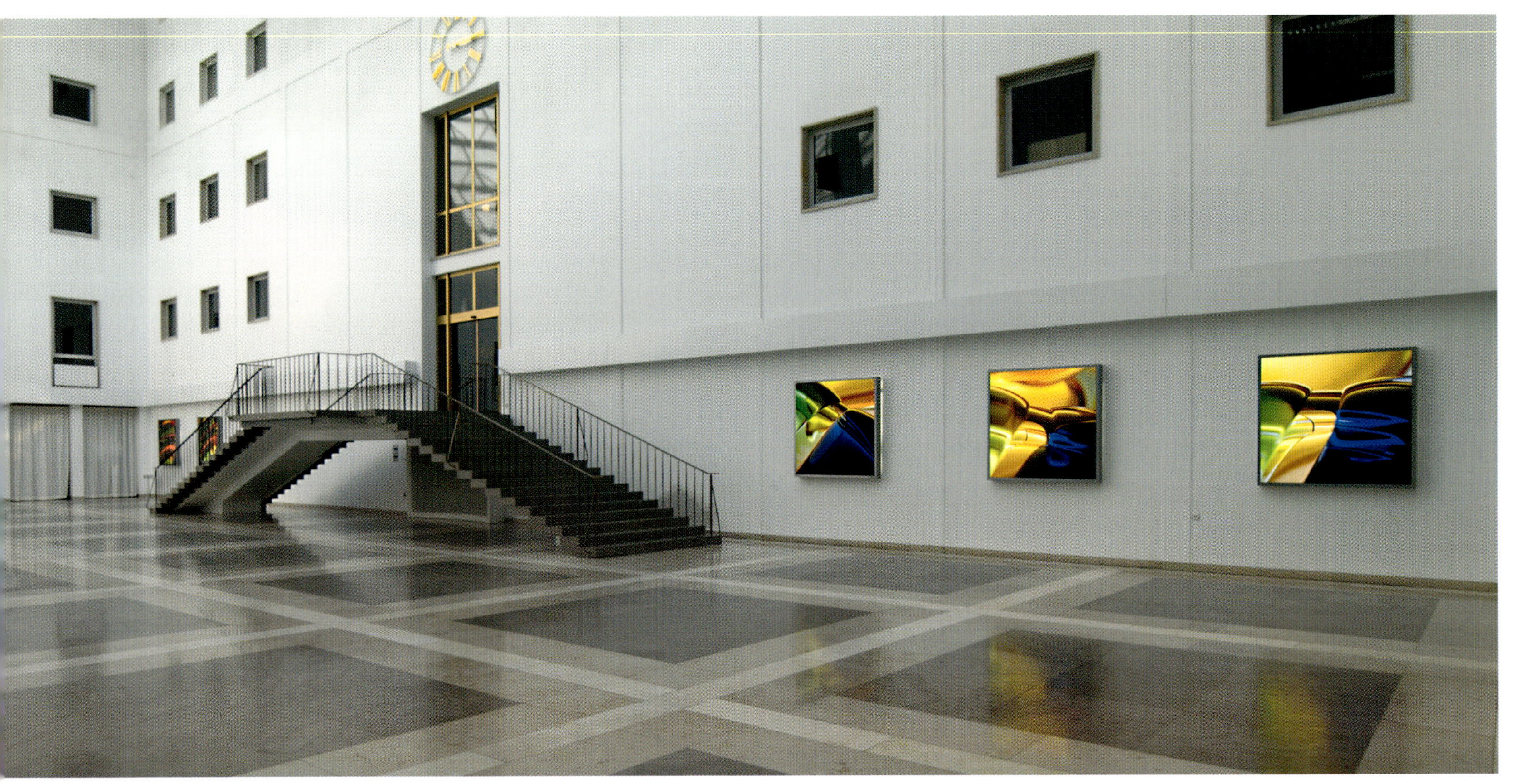

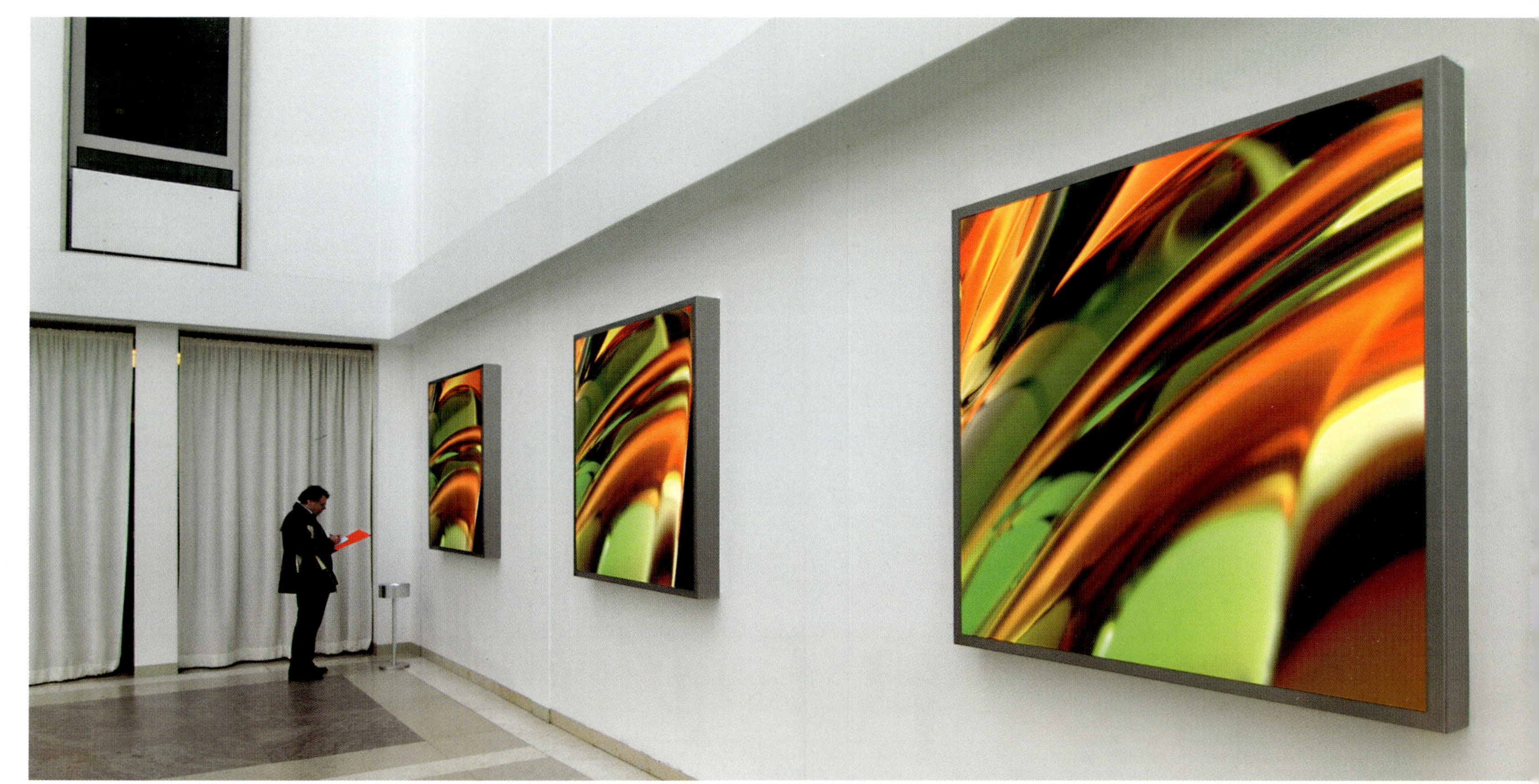

E-ON Bayern Regensburg . Administration Building . Regensburg . Germany . 2004

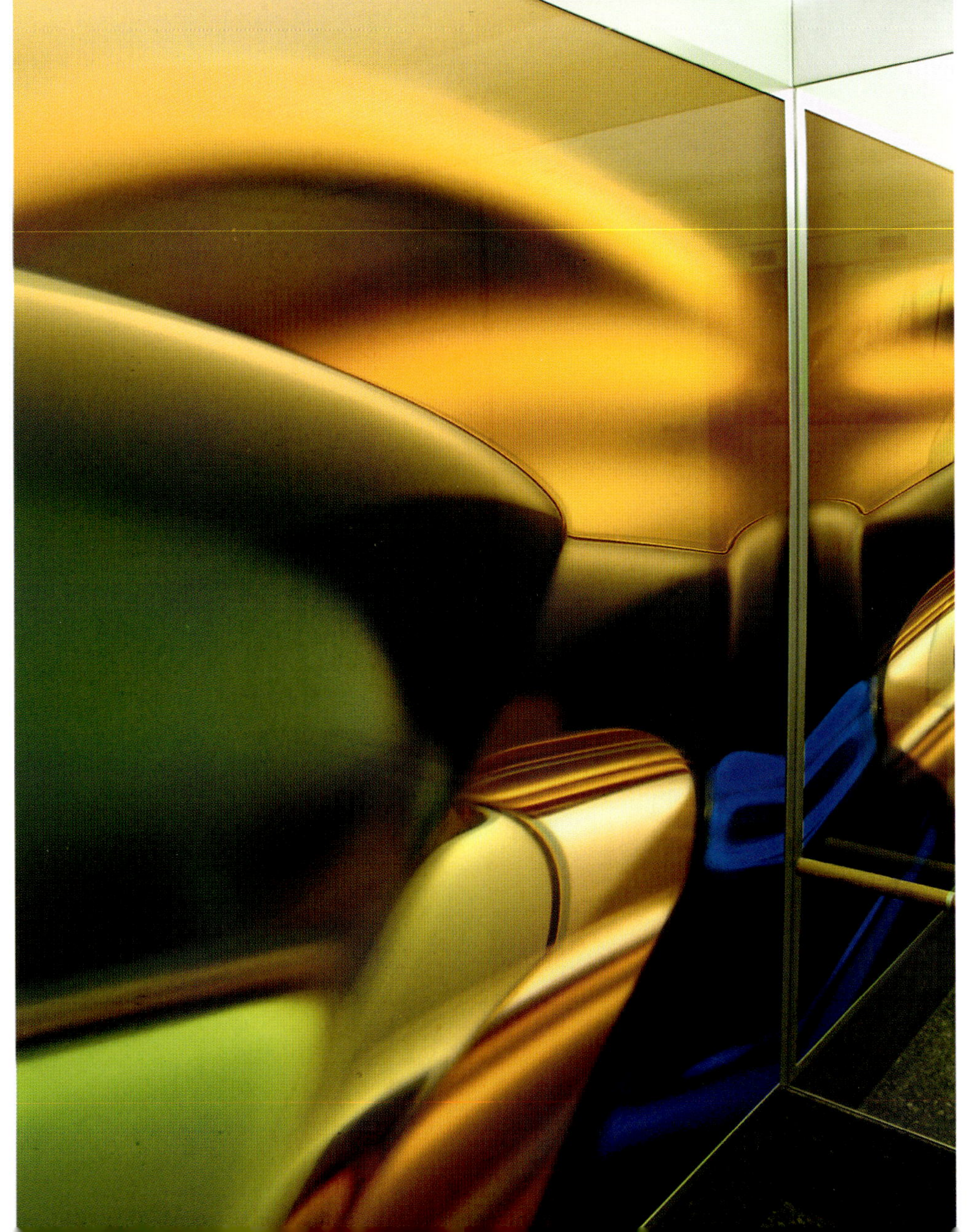

Immobilien Investment Frankfurt
Skyper . Frankfurt . Germany . 2005

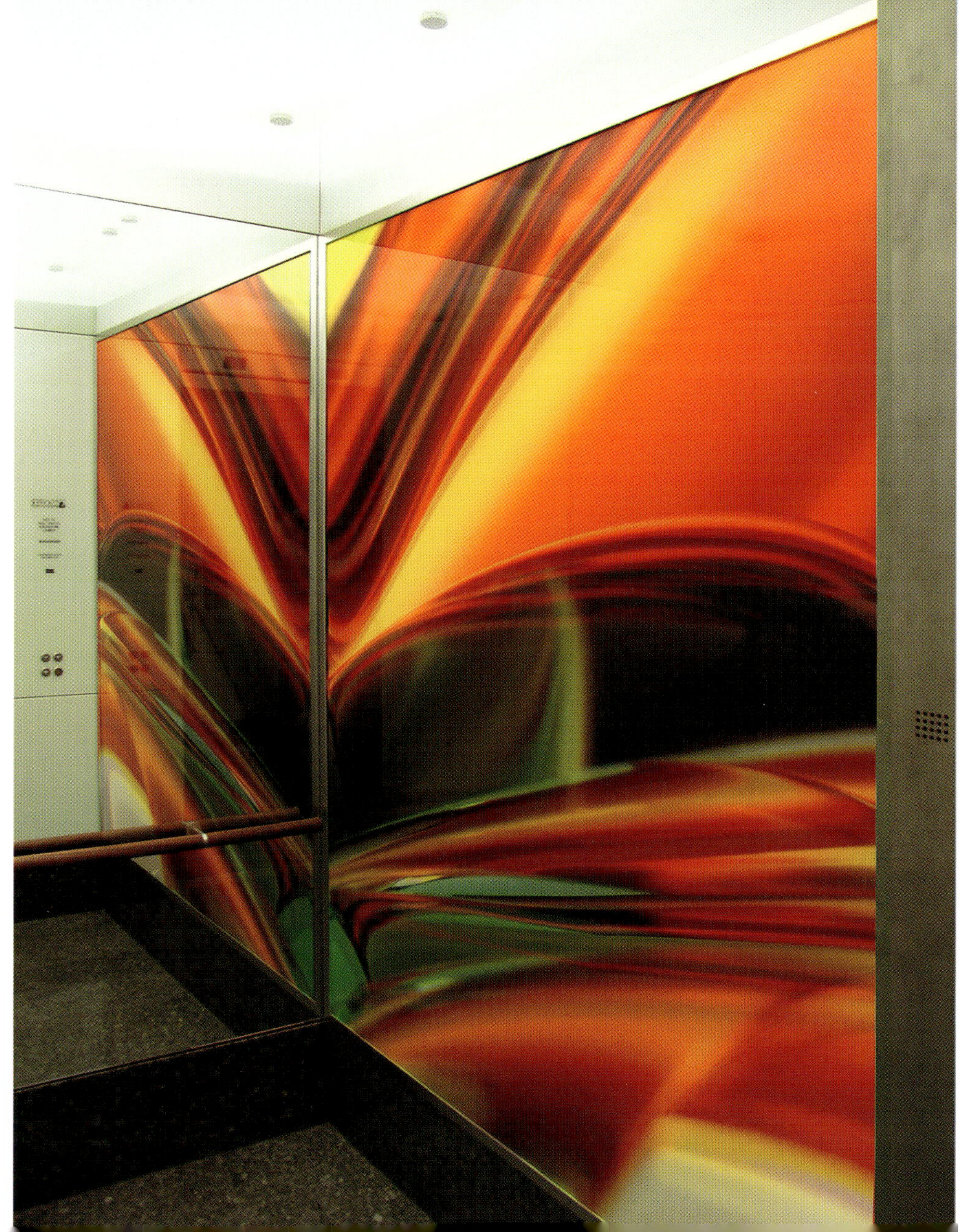

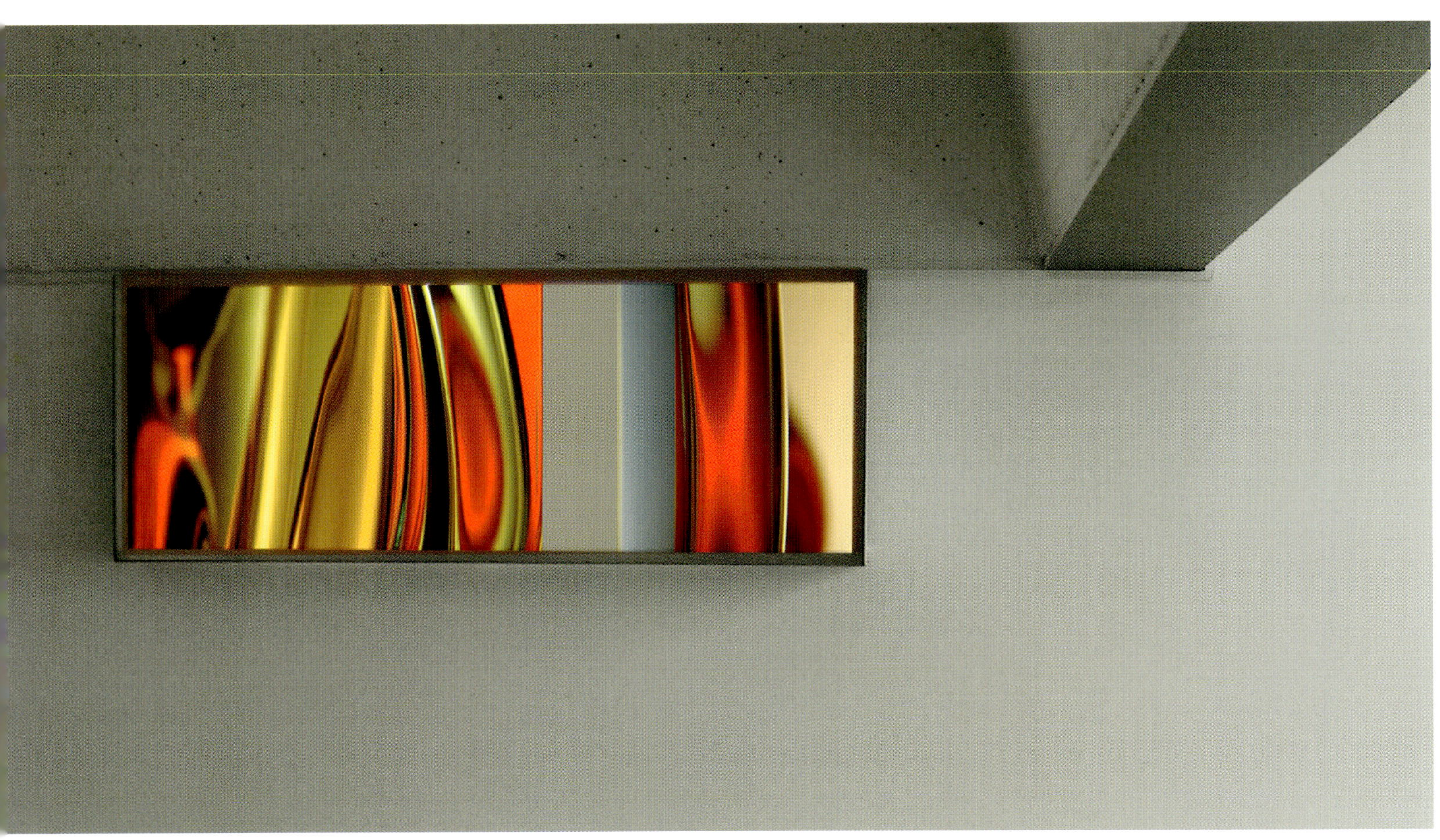

Private Collection Zurich . Switzerland . 2005

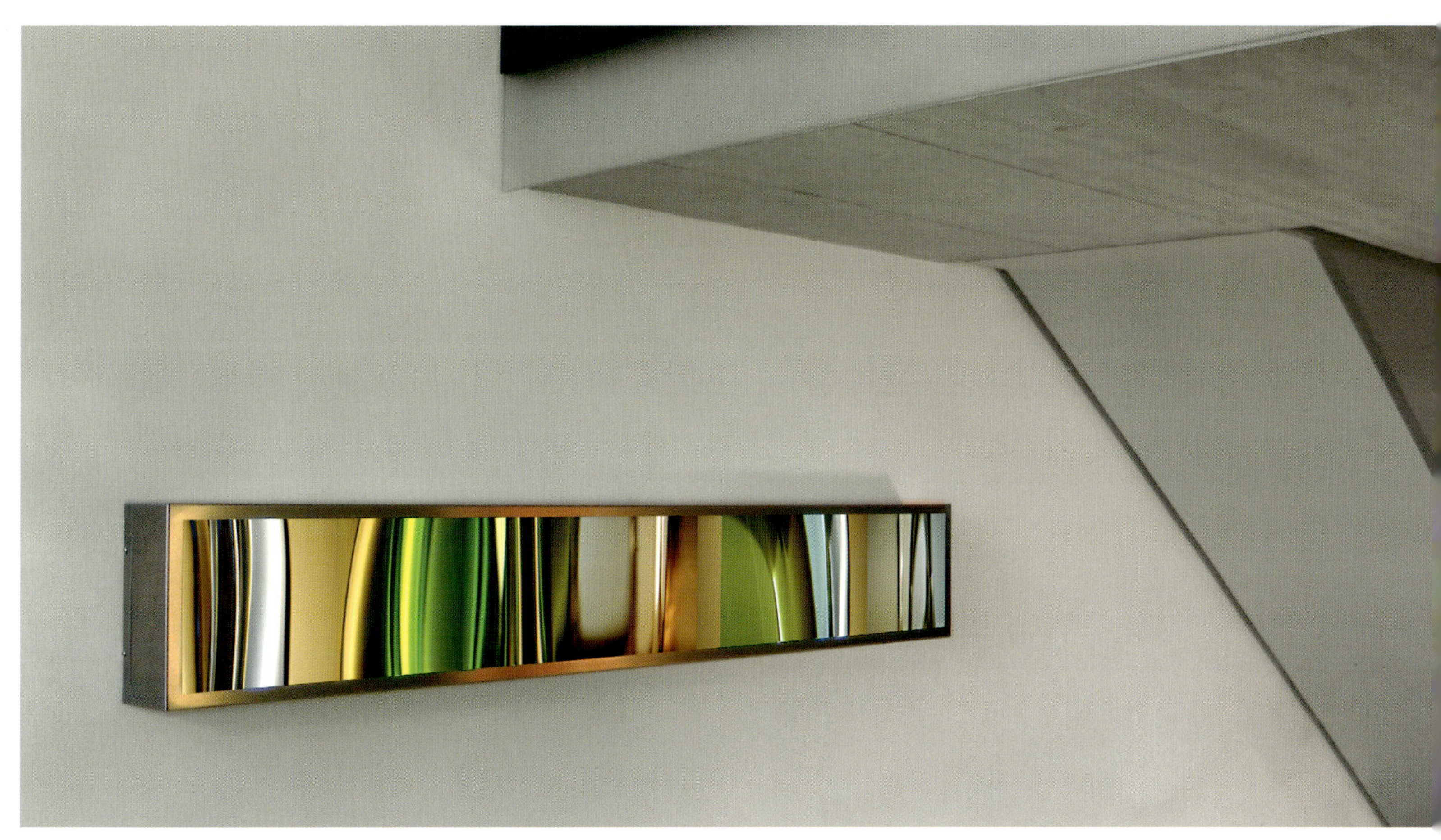

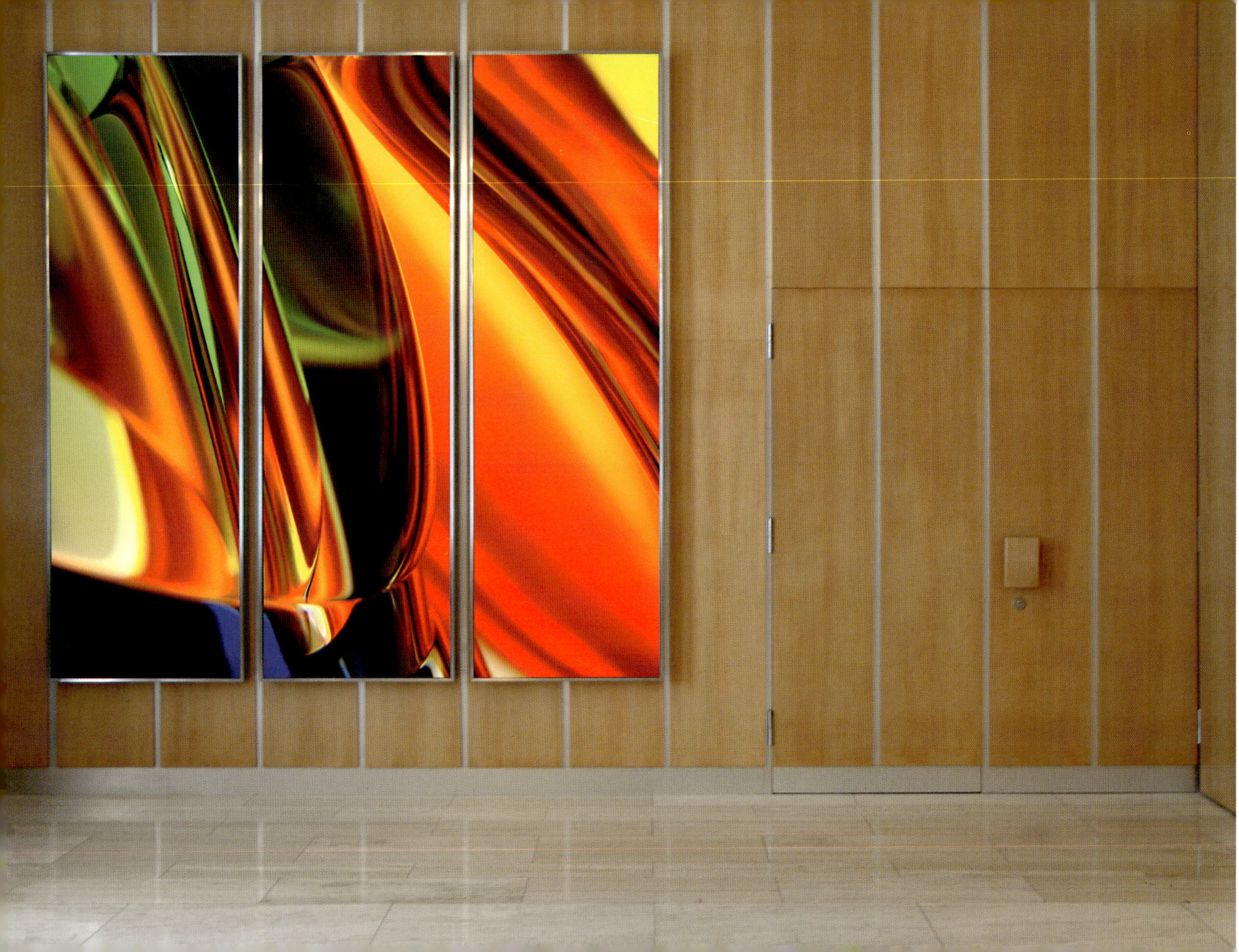

Derag AG . Hotel Kanzler . Bonn . Germany . 2005

Hotel Maximilian . Nuremberg . Germany . 2007

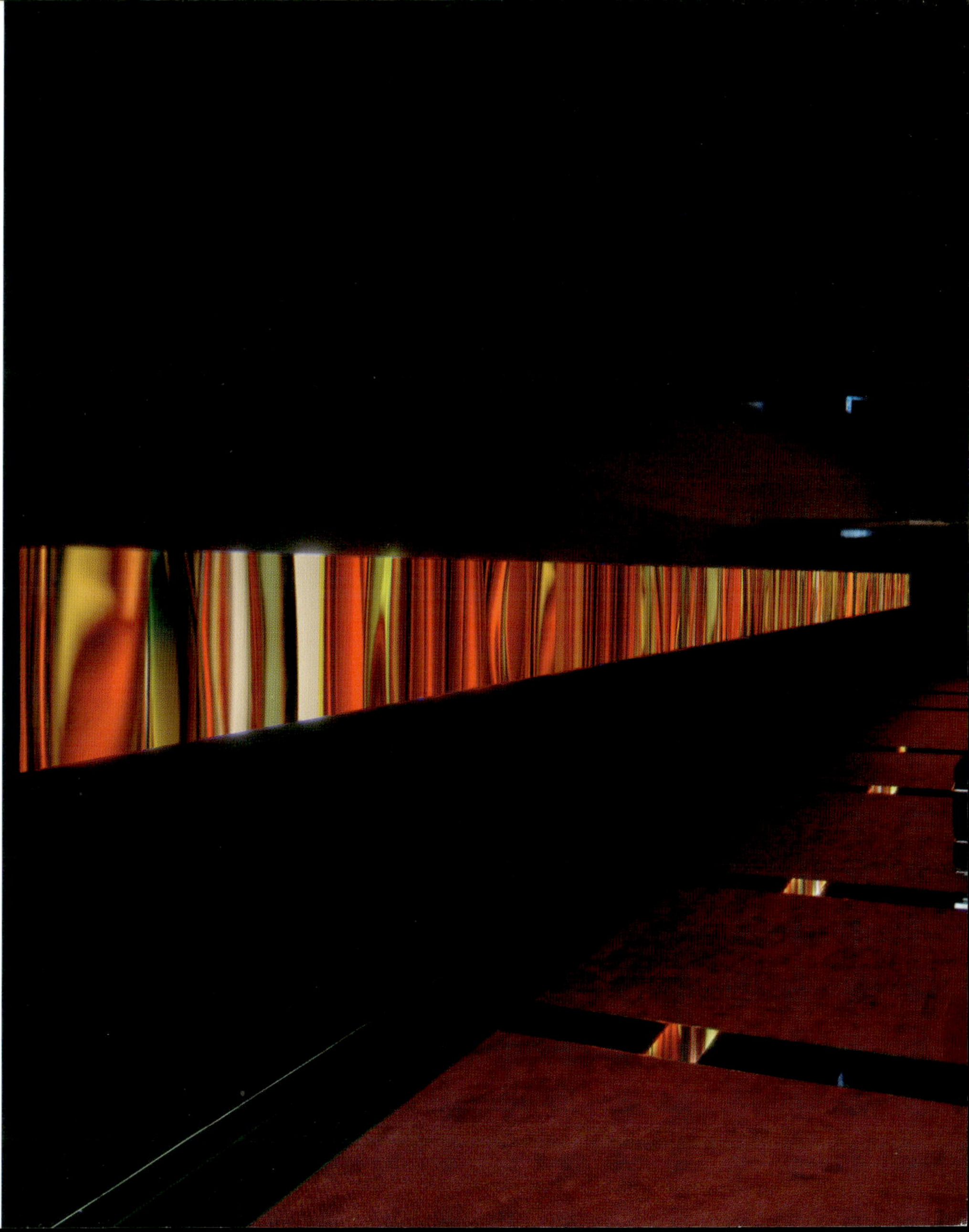

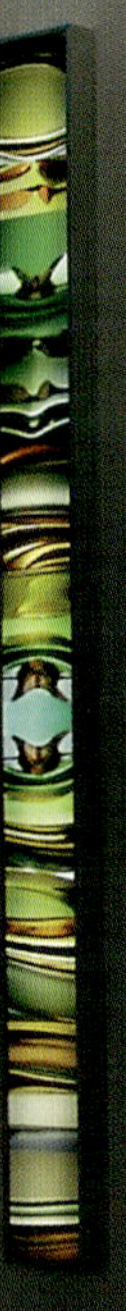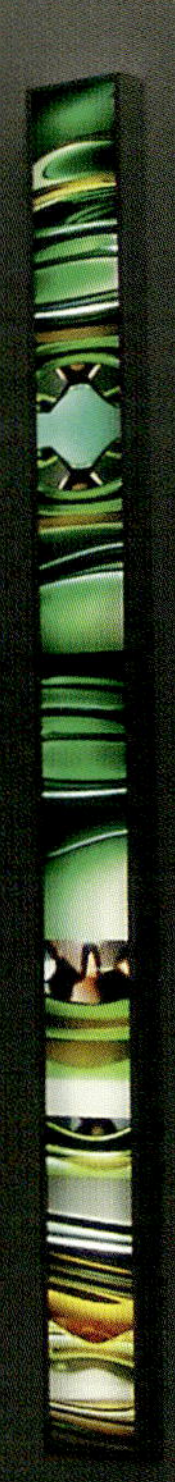

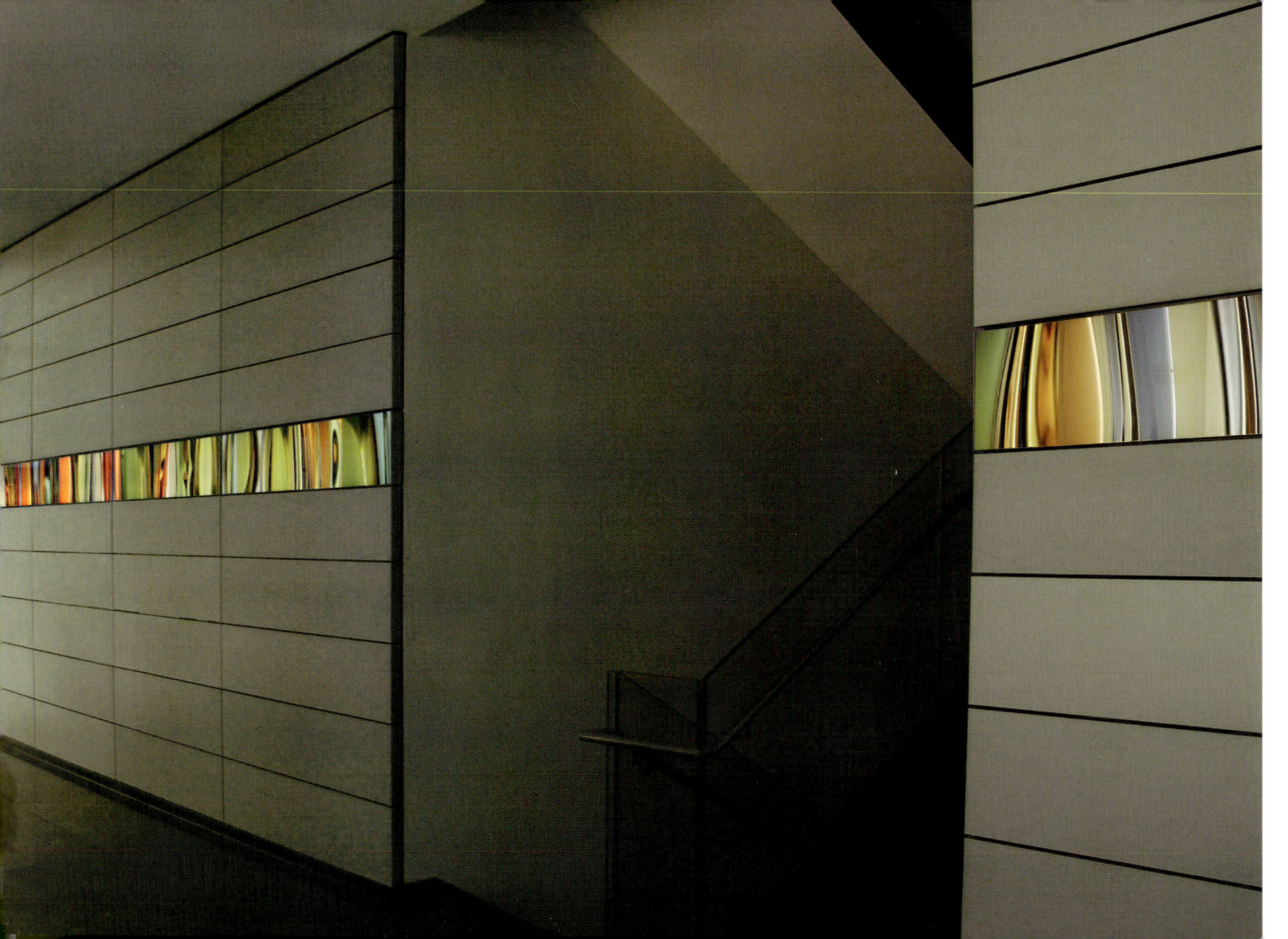

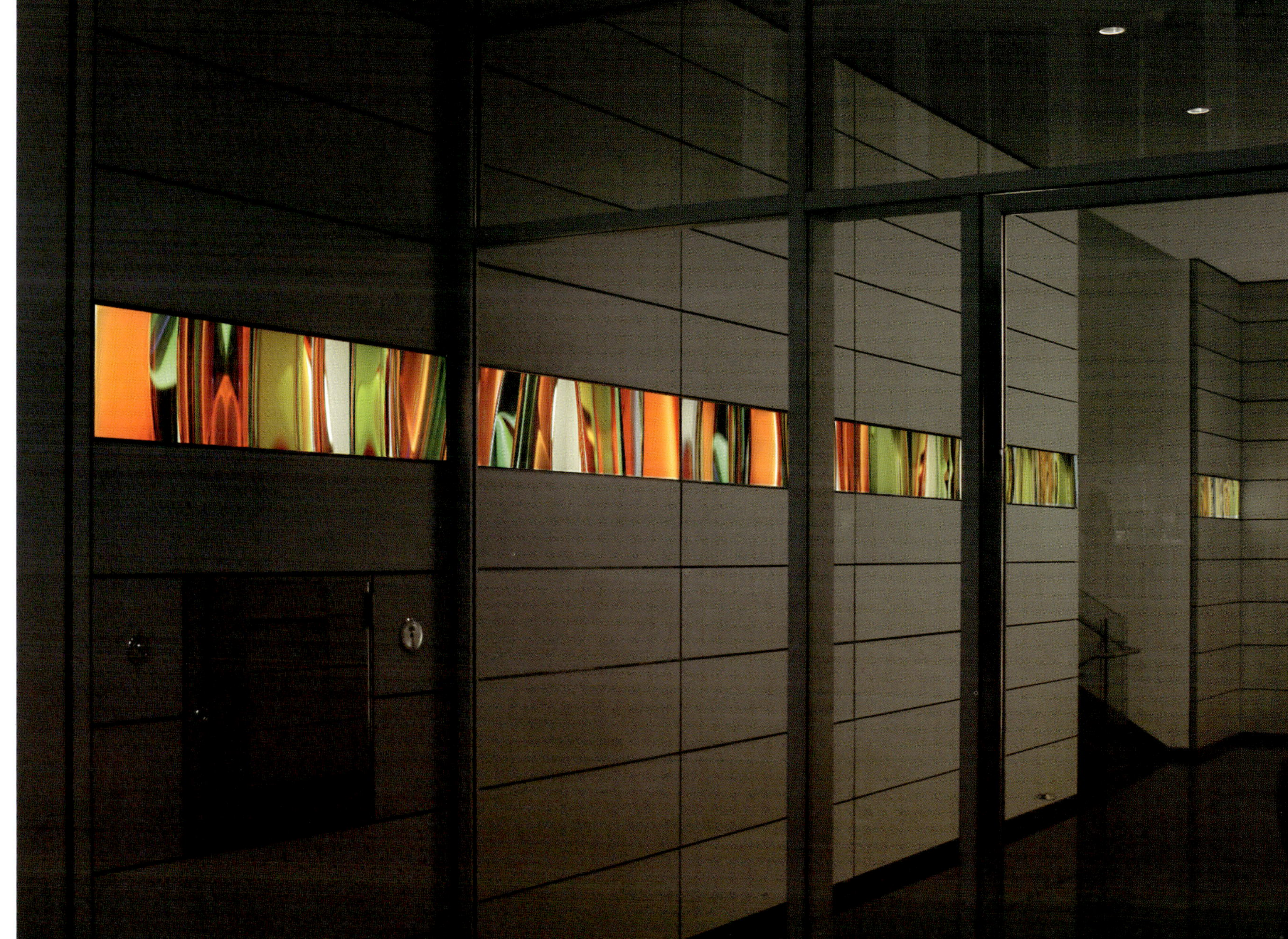

Selected Public Art

2007    **Booz Allen Hamilton GmbH** . Berlin . Germany . **2 Aluminum Light Boxes** . Laserchrome Slide on Plexiglass . Each 100 x 100 cm
   **Hotel Maximilian** . Nuremberg . Germany . **Light Box** . Laserchrome Slide on Plexiglass . 1860 x 50 cm
   **School in Bavaria** . Germany . **4 Stainless Steel Light Boxes** . Laserchrome Slide on Plexiglass . Each 125 x 125 cm

2005    **Immobilien Investment Frankfurt** . Skyper . Frankfurt . Germany . **8 elevator cars** . Laserchrome Slide on Plexiglass . Each 196 x 216 cm
   **Derag AG** . Hotel Kanzler . Bonn . Germany . **3 Stainless Steel Light Boxes** . Laserchrome Slide on Plexiglass . Each 300 x 100 cm
   **Private Collection Zurich** . Switzerland . **2 Stainless Steel Light Boxes** . Laserchrome Slide on Plexiglass . 210 x 30 cm . 140 x 50 cm

2004    **E-ON Bayern Regensburg** . Administration Building . Regensburg . Germany . **6 Stainless Steel Light Boxes** . Laserchrome Slide on Plexiglass . Each 150 x 150 cm
   **Neuga Bauträge** . Object at Burghauser-Tor . Neuötting . Germany . **4 Aluminum Light Boxes** . Laserchrome Slide on Plexiglass . Each 350 x 20 cm

2003    **DEKA Immobilien Investment Frankfurt** . Leomax . Munich . Germany . **Light Box** . Laserchrome Slide on Glass . 920 x 32 cm
   **Staatliches Hochbauamt Rosenheim** . Land Surveying Office . Germany . **4 Aluminum Light Boxes** . Laserchrome Slide on Plexiglass . Each 300 x 25 cm

1999    **Passauer Neue Presse** . Media Center . Passau . Germany . **Light Box** . Mixed Media . 150 x 50 cm . C-Print on Dibond with Diasec Face . 150 x 240 cm

1998    **Stadt Burghausen** . Community Center . Burghausen . Germany . **2 Light Boxes** . Mixed Media . Each 150 x 150 cm
   **Passauer Neue Presse** . Editorial Office . Passau . Germany . **2 Light Boxes** . Mixed Media . 150 x 150 cm . 150 x 50 cm

1997    **Wochenblatt Burghausen** . Editorial Office . Burghausen . Germany . **20 Plates** . Mixed Media . Each 88 x 88 cm

## **KUNSTLICHT**. Eine Annäherung an die Arbeiten von Hans Kotter
**von Peter Lodermeyer**

Ein Hotel in Deutschland, in Rheinnähe. Ich frage an der Rezeption, ob ich mir die Arbeit von Hans Kotter ansehen darf, von der ich gelesen habe, dass sie sich hier im Haus befindet. Der Pförtner, der sichtlich keine Ahnung hat, wovon ich rede, verweist mich vage in eines der oberen Stockwerke. Ich suche lange vergebens die Gänge ab, bis ich in einer geräumigen Nische drei große, elegant proportionierte Objekte an der holzgetäfelten Wand entdecke. Im Dämmerlicht kann ich auf den Vorderflächen nicht viel erkennen. Ich bemerke einen Lichtschalter und drücke ihn, ohne zu wissen, ob er etwas mit dem Objekt zu tun hat. Ein kurzes Aufflackern im Inneren der drei hochrechteckigen Kästen – und dann ereignet sich ein wahres Lichtwunder: Auf neun Quadratmetern Fläche erstrahlt eine Kaskade von schräg übereinander hinweg wogenden Farbformen in kraftvollem Kobaltblau, Gelb und Flaschengrün. Nach rechts hin geht die Farbigkeit ganz in ein prächtiges cognacfarbenes Leuchten über. Die durchlichteten Formen bleiben undeutbar wie in einem abstraktem Gemälde und zugleich auf eigenartige Weise real, materiell, fotografisch präzise. Sie wirken organisch bewegt – und doch sind ihre Farben so kühl, ihre Anmutung so glatt, dass sie etwas irritierend Fremdes und Unnahbares bewahren.

Wer den fotografischen Arbeiten von Hans Kotter unvorbereitet gegenübertritt, die zwischen Abstraktion und Materialität, Natürlichkeit und Künstlichkeit, technischer Perfektion und malerischer Anmutung changieren, wird unvermeidlich die Frage stellen, ob es sich dabei nicht um digital erzeugte oder verfremdete Erscheinungen handelt. Die Wahrheit ist, dass sich der Künstler mit seiner Kamera in selbstgebaute Glasprismen oder in Öltröpfchen hineinzoomt, um dort das verwirrend komplizierte Spiel von Lichtbrechung, -beugung und -reflexion zu beobachten. Bei geschickter Ausleuchtung mit verschiedenen Lichtquellen kommen im Inneren dieser transparenten Medien Formen von fremdartiger Schönheit und fulminanter Farbqualität zur Erscheinung. Schwer zu identifizierende Übergänge von lichtdurchdrungener Materie, farbigen Hintergründen und reflektierenden Oberflächen schaffen dabei Phänomene, die zwar den Eindruck des Körperhaften immer wieder erwecken, ohne ihn jedoch in fassbarer Gestalt einzulösen. So erscheinen pseudo-organische Gebilde, die wie paradoxe Pflanzen oder Landschafen aus Flüssigkeiten wirken und doch zugleich unstofflich, energetisch und im Innersten unbestimmbar bleiben. Diese Formen, die Kotter dann als lichtstarke Laserchrom-Abzüge oder als Diapositive in Leuchtkästen ausstellt, werden nicht nachträglich digital bearbeitet, sondern so präsentiert, wie sie sich seiner Kamera gezeigt haben.

Kotters Thema ist das Licht. Seine Arbeiten wenden sich stets dem Licht zu und spüren seinen unerwartetsten Wirkungen nach. Dabei bringt die Vielfalt der Lichtphänomene den Künstler dazu, sich über die gängigen Gattungsgrenzen hinweg unterschiedlichste Ausdrucksmöglichkeiten und immer neue Techniken, Materialien und Präsentationsweisen zu erschließen. Hans Kotter konstruiert nicht nur Leuchtkästen, sondern baut Objekte, gießt Fundgegenstände in transparentes Kunstharz, markiert ganze Räume mit Lichtpfaden aus Leuchtfolie und nähert sich mit der Fotokamera den subtilsten Lichterscheinungen. Seine Fotoarbeiten bezeichnet er im Gespräch als „Malerei mit Licht" und weist darauf hin, dass er das Hilfsmittel der Fotografie nur auf Umwegen und eher zufällig für sich entdeckte. Kotter ist in erster Linie nicht Fotograf, sondern Lichtkünstler und als solcher unvermeidlich Raumkünstler, denn Raum erschließt sich uns visuell nur als lichthaltige Leere. Nicht nur seine Rauminstallationen, auch seine von Neonröhren erhellten Leuchtkästen zeigen eine stark in den Raum hineinwirkende und ihn verändernde Präsenz. Daher verwundert es nicht, dass er immer wieder Aufträge für großformatige Installationen im öffentlichen Raum bzw. in Firmengebäuden erhält.

Es ist überaus interessant, dass im Zusammenhang mit diesen Leuchtkästen vergleichend auf die Glasfenster der gotischen Kathedralen verwiesen wurde. Das Diaphane, d.h. das vom Licht Durchdrungenwerden transparenter Materie, sowie die Durchlichtung des Raumes galten in der Kunstgeschichte oft als Ausdruck mittelalterlicher Lichtmetaphysik. Der Zauber des Diaphanen beschäftigt gewiss auch Hans Kotter in seinen fotografischen Untersuchungen, doch darf nicht übersehen werden, dass der Künstler sich der tiefen Profanierung unseres heutigen Bezugs zum Licht durchaus bewusst ist. Er verliert sich bei seinen Ausflügen in den optischen Mikrokosmos nicht in der abstrakten Schönheit der beobachteten Lichtwirkungen. Dazu ist er zu sehr kritischer Zeitgenosse, der genau weiß, dass die im abendländischen Denken verankerten Vorstellungen über das Licht als Symbole des Göttlichen, der Wahrheit und der Vernunft längst einer tiefgreifender Säkularisierung und schließlich drastischen Trivialisierung unterzogen wurden. Eine der Voraussetzungen der abendländischen Lichtmetaphysik war sicher die weitgehende Unverfügbarkeit der Sonne in ihrem natürlichen Tages- und Jahreslauf. Mit der Elektrizität wurde Licht zu einer ständig verfügbaren, erzeugbaren und manipulierbaren Größe. Kunstlicht ist für uns alle zu einer selbstverständlichen Voraussetzung des modernen Alltags geworden. Noch die hässlichste Stadt hat in der Nacht im Schein der Leuchtreklamen, Autoscheinwerfer und Straßenlampen teil an der profanen Magie des Kunstlichts. Spätestens mit Dan Flavins Installationen aus Leuchtstoffröhren in den 60er Jahren ist das Kunstlicht zugleich Thema und „Material" eines neuen künstlerischen Genres, der Lichtkunst, geworden.

In Kotters Installationen und seinen Leuchtkästen wirken die durchlichteten Formen und spiegelglatten Objekte stets „sauber glänzend rein", wie der selbstironische Titel einer Ausstellung von 1999 lautete. Schon dieses wie ein Werbespruch klingende Motto kann daran erinnern, dass die abendländische Lichtmetaphysik heute in die Hände des Produktdesigns und der Werbung mit ihren fragwürdigen Glücksversprechungen gefallen ist. Wir alle kennen die Werbefilme, in denen immerzu die Sonne scheint und jede Fliese, jede chrom- und lackversiegelte Oberfläche aufblitzt, die Gebisse kariesfrei in hygienischer Makellosigkeit erstrahlen und die metalliclackierten Limousinen wie Wesen aus höheren Welten lautlos und in blitzblanker Schönheit durchs Bild jagen. Hans Kotters Werke platzieren sich optisch bewusst in verführerischer, fast koketter Nähe zu den ebenso perfekten wie sterilen Erzeugnissen der Warenästhetik. Leuchtkästen, wie Kotter sie verwendet, sind uns außerhalb des Kunstkontextes vor allem als Werbemittel aus Kaufhäusern und Modeboutiquen bekannt. Und in seiner Installation „The very Best ..." lässt er Alltagsobjekte aus der Sportwelt, eine Tischtennisplatte und Vereinspokale, in kalter, materialbetonter Pracht erglänzen. Indem er das glatte Design durch die Lichtinszenierung noch verfremdend übertreibt, gewinnen die Objekte eine ironische Übersteigerung, die sie zu „coolen" Zeichen ihrer selbst ohne jeden Gebrauchswert mutieren lässt. Die Fetischisierung von Ästhetik wird erfahrbar in der Unbespielbarkeit der transparenten, von unten her beleuchteten Tischtennisplatte. Deren Abmessungen entsprechen zwar exakt den geforderten Turniermaßen, jedoch enthält die Platte ein Wasser-Öl-Gemisch, auf dem ein realer Tischtennisball sofort haften bliebe. Unbenutzbarkeit als Preis für die Schönheit? Kotter lotet mit seinen Arbeiten den schmalen Grat zwischen Kunst und Design, zwischen Schönheit und Funktionalität aus. Auch seine an die Wand gehängten oder gelehnten Leuchtkästen schwanken zwischen dem Status als minimalistische Plastik und schickem Designobjekt. Doch sobald man die in ihrem Inneren verborgenen Leuchtröhren aktiviert, werden sie zu Laternae magicae, die uns betörende Bilder aus der Wunderwelt des Lichts zeigen. Kotters Arbeiten sind Etüden über die unversiegbare Faszination des Lichts.

## Selected Group Exhibition

2007    **ArtMbassy** . Berlin . Germany . Obsession through Technique    **Istituto Italiano di Cultura** . Cologne . Germany . Suitcas    **Kinetica Museum** . London . In the Flux
**Kunstverein Aschaffenburg** . Germany . Best Before …

2006    **Kinetica Museum** . London . Life Forms    **Rosenbaum Contemporary** . Boca Raton . Florida . Fire and Ice

2005    **Gallery Kashya Hildebrand** . Geneva . Switzerland . Reflections    **Gallery Bernd Lausberg** . Düsseldorf . Germany . Rot als Farbe [Red as Colour]
**Gallery Kashya Hildebrand** . New York . Spectrum    **Berlinerkunst Project** . NY Arts Magazine . Berlin . Look!    **Gallery Kashya Hildebrand** . Zurich . Solaris

2003    **Backfabrik** . Berlin . Germany . Lichtung II [Galde II]

2001    **Oberbayerische Kulturtage Altötting** . Germany . Kraft und Magie [Power and Magic]

2000    **Kulturmodell Passau** . Germany    **Haus der Kunst** . Munich . Germany . Große Kunstausstellung    **Städtische Galerie im Park** . Viersen . Germany

1999    **Museum of Modern Art** . New York . Online Exhibition The Museum as Muse: Artist Reflect    **Monique Goldstrom Gallery** . New York . Snapshots

1998    **Abraham Lubelski Gallery** . New York . Country without Borders    **Neue Galerie Oberhausmuseum** . Passau . Germany

1997    **Old Tax Office** . Rosenheim . Germany . Keine Erinnerung [No Memory]    **Casa Gallery** . Tokyo . Japan . The Power of Words and Signs
**Index Gallery** . Osaka . Japan    **Abraham Lubelski Gallery** . New York    **Kultur Modell Passau** . Metamorphosia    **Biennale New York** . NY Arts Magazine

1996    **450 Broadway Gallery** . New York . Sonic Identity

1997    **Stadtmuseum Waldkraiburg** . Germany . Annual Art Exhibition    **Dariusz Gubala Gallery** . New York . Cyber Culture

1993    **Dariusz Gubala Gallery** . New York . Vertigo Art    **Madelyn Jordon Gallery** . New York


## Art Fairs

Arte Fiera Bologna . Art Forum Berlin . Art Moscow . Art Toronto . Art Fair Cologne . Art Miami . Palm Beach 3 . Kunst Zurich . Art Frankfurt .
Scope Art Fair London . MiArt Milan . Kunst Köln

## Hans Kotter

**1966** born in Mühldorf am Inn . Germany   **1993/94** Art Students League [Membership] . New York with Bruce Dorfman und William Scharf
**2004** Culture Award E-ON Bayern AG . Germany   **lives and works** in Berlin


## Selected Solo Exhibitions

2008   **Gallery Bernd Lausberg** . Toronto . Colour Rush

2007   **Patrick Heide Contemporary Art** . London . Colour Rush and Blue Line

2006   **Luminale Frankfurt** . with Patrick Heide Contemporary Art . London   **Gallery Bernd Lausberg** . Düsseldorf . Light Colour Room

2005   **Berlinische Galerie** with Spectral . Chromatic Impulse

2004   **Raum für Kunst** . Kunstverein Ravensburg . Germany . Balance   **Aedes Berlin** . Germany . Illuminations
       **Patrick Heide Contemporary Art** . London . Macro Landscape   **Scope Art Fair** . London . TV Shot

2003   **Patrick Heide Contemporary Art** . Frankfurt . Germany . Lichtecht [Lightfast]

2002   **Bezirks Galerie** . Bezirk Oberbayern . Munich . Germany . Light and Colour   **Stadtmuseum Neuötting** . Germany . Beauty in Plastic

2001   **Pasinger Fabrik** . Munich . Germany . Blue Line

1999   **Gallery Benden & Klimczak** . Cologne . Germany . Stillleben [Still Life]

1998   **Städtische Galerie im Haus der Kultur** . Waldkraiburg . Germany . Spurensicherung

1997   **Modern Theatre Munich** . Germany . Diary with Sound-Collage   **Galllery Hofmeisterhaus** . Massing/Rottal . Tagebuchnotizen

1994   **Radiocenter of Bratislava** . Slovakia . Body Language

1993   **Stadtmuseum Waldkraiburg** . Germany   **Chuck Levitan Gallery** . New York . Daydreams

# Imprint

**Editor** . Herausgeber . **Patrick Heide Contemporary Art** . www.patrickheide.com
**Graphic Design** . Gestaltung . **# B_UTOP  b:uro d.es_senses** . www.b-utop.de

**Text** . Text . **Peter Lodermeyer** . www.lodermeyer.com
**Translation** . Übersetzung . **Elizabeth Volk**

**Photo Credits** . Fotonachweis . **Erwino Nitz** . **Wolfgang Claus** . **Hans Kotter**
**Print** . Druck . **Lanzinger Medien** . www.lanzinger.org

**Edition** . Auflage . **450**
**All rights reserved** . Alle Rechte vorbehalten . © 2007 Patrick Heide Contemporary Art
Printed in Germany

**ISBN**  978-0-9745148-7-1

**Published by** . Verlag . **GlobalArtAffairs Publishing** . New York . USA . www.globalartaffairs.com
**Distributed by** . Vertrieb . **Cornerhouse Publications** . Manchester . England . www.cornerhouse.org/books

**Patrick Heide Contemporary Art**
11 Church Street
London NW8 8EE, UK
T +44 (0)20 7724 5548
info@patrickheide.com
**www.patrickheide.com**